Freemasonry: A Very Short Introduction

VERY SHORT INTRODUCTIONS are for anyone wanting a stimulating and accessible way into a new subject. They are written by experts, and have been translated into more than 45 different languages.

The series began in 1995, and now covers a wide variety of topics in every discipline. The VSI library now contains over 500 volumes—a Very Short Introduction to everything from Psychology and Philosophy of Science to American History and Relativity—and continues to grow in every subject area.

Very Short Introductions available now:

Available soon:

For more information visit our website

www.oup.com/vsi/

Andreas Önnerfors

FREEMASONRY

A Very Short Introduction

OXFORD
UNIVERSITY PRESS

Great Clarendon Street, Oxford, OX2 6DP,
United Kingdom

Oxford University Press is a department of the University of Oxford.
It furthers the University's objective of excellence in research, scholarship,
and education by publishing worldwide. Oxford is a registered trade mark of
Oxford University Press in the UK and in certain other countries

© Andreas Önnerfors 2017

The moral rights of the author have been asserted

First edition published in 2017

Published in the United States of America by Oxford University Press
198 Madison Avenue, New York, NY 10016, United States of America

British Library Cataloguing in Publication Data
Data available

Library of Congress Control Number: 2017935045

ISBN 978-0-19-879627-5

Printed and bound by
CPI Group (UK) Ltd, Croydon, CR0 4YY

Contents

Acknowledgements

Freemasonry is a topic that occupies a challenged place in societal debate and it has been truly rewarding to work on this subject, it being a research interest that I have pursued for about fifteen years. Although my ambition was to touch on most aspects of freemasonry seen during the last three centuries of its development, inevitably I have had to be selective in terms of producing a Very Short Introduction on the subject.

I am extremely grateful for discussions on different aspects of freemasonry with friends and colleagues at a number of occasions and would like to thank particularly: Henrik Bogdan, Marcel van Ackeren, Jürgen Müller, Mikael Shainkman, Peter Lind, Frances Zetterberg, and Ola Wikander as well as two anonymous readers from Oxford University Press. Special thanks to Frank Langenaken and François Rognon, for granting permission for reproduction of images from the collections of CEDOM/MADOC (Brussels) and GLDF (Paris); and to the BNF (Paris) for smooth collaboration on image sourcing.

Writing this book would have been impossible without the support of the Alfried-Krupp-Wissenschaftskolleg in Greifswald on the shores of the Baltic Sea, where I spent a sabbatical in the summer of 2016—and where the azure horizon eternally blurs the boundaries between heaven and earth.

List of illustrations

List of abbreviations

(These are only listed if used in multiple places throughout the book.)

AASR	Ancient and Accepted Scottish Rite 33° (1801), divided on US-territory in the Northern (NJ) and Southern Jurisdiction (SJ).
GAOTU	Grand or Great Architect of the Universe, the 'supreme being' referred to in masonic ideology.
GODF	Grand Orient de France (1738/72).
UGLE	United Grand Lodge of England and Wales (1717/1813).

Chapter 1
Two approaches to freemasonry

This book examines how and why, since its inception in Britain, men (and women) have organized themselves socially and voluntarily within freemasonry over the course of three centuries, despite very divergent cultural and political settings worldwide. There is no single definition or form of freemasonry, which is why contemporary scholars prefer to speak of 'freemasonries'. Indeed, the brotherhood and its history are surrounded by an abundance of facts and fictions and sources, which this book aims to clarify, enabling the reader to navigate this complex subject matter. The common view of freemasonry tends to fall into one of two main camps: idealization or distrust.

Idealization

Take for instance Pierre Bezukhov, the hero of Tolstoy's world-famous novel *War and Peace* (1869): in the middle of Pierre's restless soul-searching he encounters a wise old man. The stranger tells Pierre that his life is a 'regrettable delusion' and that joining freemasonry promises purification. Conscience and reason will guide the seeker to perfection. In the Russian capital, St Petersburg at the time, Pierre isolates himself reading devotional literature and starts to 'believe in the possibility of the brotherhood of men united in the aim of supporting one another in the path of virtue'. Finally he is recruited into the local lodge (the smallest organizational unit of freemasonry). To become a freemason, Pierre has to be initiated through a ritual (just as millions like him in reality have been) and is exposed to questions and tests.

In Tolstoy's novel, the candidate is blindfolded and led by a guide to a room of reflection furnished with signs of death and mortality like a skull and a coffin. Here an officer of the lodge questions Pierre about his intentions to join freemasonry and he replies that he desires regeneration. Asked about his conception of the brotherhood, Pierre responds, 'I imagine that freemasonry is the fraternity and equality of men who have virtuous aims'. The officer reveals the aims of the masonic order (tradition of mystery, self-purification and self-perfection, improvement of mankind) and presents a catalogue of its major virtues (discretion, obedience, morality, love of humanity, courage, generosity, and the love of death). Last but not least, Pierre is told that freemasonry informs its members not only in words but also by other means, and that symbols are used to communicate something 'not cognizable by the senses'. Finally, Pierre is guided to the doorsteps of the lodge, which is also the name of the physical meeting place of freemasons throughout the world. Here, an intricate ritual of initiation unfolds at the end of which Pierre takes an oath of allegiance and is ultimately allowed to see the light—the blindfold is released.

I have started with this account for a good reason. The way into the brotherhood, which Tolstoy describes, is one of the unique features of freemasonry as a Western initiatory society and a ritual community with its own secret symbolism and methods, performed as a walk from darkness to light. We do not know how Tolstoy received knowledge about freemasonry, but the parts in *War and Peace* that describe Russian freemasonry at the time are quite accurate when compared with contemporary sources. There have been millions of men and a sizeable number of women who have become freemasons worldwide over the last three centuries, all in a similar manner to Pierre. The motives for joining are of course always individual. In Pierre's fictional case, freemasonry promised guidance in his dissatisfied life that would lead towards improvement and perfection. The masonic lodge is the place where this ideal of moral refinement is offered to the individual candidate and where it is experienced in fraternity.

But Tolstoy also hints at a larger purpose of freemasonry (we might call it cosmopolitan and philanthropic): to develop a charitable responsibility for humanity as a whole. How this is achieved in the best way has been a cause of division within freemasonry for at least two centuries. Should freemasonry take an active role in shaping the society in which it is embedded? Or should its sole influence be confined to its individual members, who in their larger society act as individuals who are united by shared values and refined morality? This touches upon another aspect of freemasonry present since its inception, namely its views on the interrelation of politics and society, and this eventually caused an internal schism in freemasonry in the second half of the 19th century.

In a key scene of *War and Peace*, Pierre develops a political agenda for freemasonry. He is immediately accused by his lodge brothers of having crossed a boundary that places him in line with the infamous Bavarian 'Illuminati' (1776–85). The Order of Illuminati is a secret and later prohibited masonic-like society in late 18th-century Germany that pushed for societal reforms, which from today's perspective appear fairly moderate. Still, the 'Illuminati' to this day fire popular imagination. And the prominence placed on secrecy, opacity, and confidentiality in freemasonry mean that it was from the start at odds with authorities, secular as well as sacred. Its organizational form is open to abuse. Freemasonry was eventually outlawed in Russia in 1822 exactly for these reasons—the peak moment of a trend that had started in Europe with repeated papal condemnations in the 1700s and the rise of the idea of conspiracy in conservative and reactionary politics following the French Revolution (see Figure 1).

1. Poster of the French anti-masonic movie *Forces Occultes* (1943).

Distrust

During the 1790s freemasonry and other groups were accused of undermining social order and promoting revolutionary change. Influenced by public opinion, in 1799 the British parliament adopted a 'Secret Societies' Act', which controlled the activities of masonic lodges in Britain until 1967. About two decades later, two investigative book titles appeared on the British book market, *The Brotherhood* (1983) and later *Inside the Brotherhood* (1989), followed up by a TV documentary. The claim was made that freemasonry interferes in significant sectors of society, particularly within politics, the police, and courts of law.

One of the backdrops to the success of these books was a political turmoil in Italy caused by the criminal activities of a lodge in Italy, Propaganda Due (P2), which was hijacked by a mafia-like secret network. The claim of both books is that freemasonry occupies a significant place in many sectors of British society (predominantly the police force) encouraging nepotism and corruption and potential covering-up of unlawful activities. In so far as it is possible to count religion in Britain as an integral part of social life, both titles cemented the centuries-old argument that freemasonry is incompatible with Christianity. In the last chapter of *The Brotherhood*, the author used the polarization of the Cold War conflict, the fact that Britain was at war with Argentina, and the topicality of the events surrounding the Italian lodge P2 to claim that freemasonry, as a tool of Soviet secret politics, posed a substantial danger to Britain. Six years later, after the collapse of the Iron Curtain, such a point was of course void of meaning; however, the insinuations expressed in both books still are plentiful. It is worth noting that they called for an official government investigation to be carried out in the UK, and also concluded that membership of public servants in a secret society such as freemasonry should be banned. A similar argument had already been expressed in governmental prohibitions and regulations against secret societies across Europe from around 1800. The vocabulary of both books is rife with scandalizing terms like 'undermine', 'conspiracy', 'corruption', and 'manipulation' that have been voiced in anti-masonic discourse ever since. The stories had all the ingredients of a real-life political thriller of Cold War proportions, with KGB intervention, money laundering, assassinations, and evil machinations. The anti-masonic theme of these books eventually percolated down to popular fiction such as an episode of *Inspector Morse*, 'Masonic Mysteries', screened in 1990, where Morse's disdain for freemasonry and its influence upon the police force is laid open.

And, just as after the French Revolution, the issue stirred up public opinion in the United Kingdom, leading to a parliamentary inquiry: in 1997 the two-volume Home Affairs Committee report 'Freemasonry in the Police and Judiciary' appeared, which was followed up two years later by 'Freemasonry in Public Life'. As a result, between 1998 and 2009, the Home Office adopted a policy of demanding disclosure of masonic membership for all successful candidates for judicial appointment. The legislation was eventually withdrawn because of its incompatibility with European human rights standards. However, secrecy and public life always make for an uneasy mix. The decline in the status of freemasonry in England in the 1990s was in part a consequence of the role freemasons had appeared to play in some high profile miscarriages of justice. The relationship between the police, the legal and political establishment, and freemasons is complicated, raising further questions about the extent to which the esoteric side of freemasonry is divorced from public life.

An important thing to note with both Home Affairs Committee reports is, however, how much they are concerned with (despite the lack of credible evidence) the public's negative view of freemasonry, the 'general feeling of unease', or the 'widespread belief that improper masonic influence does play a part in public life', which potentially undermines public confidence in public institutions. This might also point to larger issues such as disturbed relations between perceived societal elites and ordinary citizens, existential fears that important decisions are taken in opaque zones of informal economies beyond electoral influence. Psychologically, as Swiss sociologist Georg Simmel (1906) pointed out, this is a matter of trust. To allow secrecy is a measurement of confidence in interpersonal and societal relations. Secrecy, he claimed, is 'one of the greatest accomplishments of humanity'.

Striking a balance

I have deliberately set out this book with two very opposed but representative images of freemasonry. One image, as in Tolstoy's story, idealizes the fraternity and its values, their impact upon introverted personal development and extroverted charity. The other, as found in popular perception and governmental policies, takes a critical view of secrecy and sees it as a threat to society and transparency in government. These views are typical representations of common and polarized perceptions, depending on the angle from which the topic of freemasonry is approached.

Some people arrive at the subject through the kind of idealization we can read in Pierre's life-changing encounter with the brotherhood, others search on the Internet, where among the tens of thousands of search results, the negative image of conspiracy overwhelmingly prevails. Some images, as perceived by practising freemasons, are shaped by the positive experience of internally communicated knowledge; others, as perceived by outsiders, are the result of a more critical stance.

This book will, in contrast with both of these positions, explore freemasonry from a less biased position, drawing on a growing body of research that has been produced over the course of the last two decades. Pioneered by academics in Europe and the USA and with a new availability of historical sources, major progress has been achieved in the academic study of freemasonry. And only solid facts can help to strike a balance between idealization and distrust. A basic chronology will be provided to enable the reader to place the themes of subsequent chapters within time and space. Furthermore, I will outline which religious and philosophical ideas in the Western tradition have shaped the worldview of freemasonry. Closely related to the ideas circulating in freemasonry, the experience of ritual and initiation forms the distinctive methodological centrepiece of masonic education. Freemasonry as a voluntary association also developed a specific organizational culture that will be explained. Although in principle freemasonry promotes tolerance, openness, and inclusion, from its inception issues of exclusion based upon gender, race, and religion have collided with its pretensions towards universality. Female freemasonry, rarely touched upon in general overviews, will be treated extensively. Finally, the relationship of freemasonry with the outside world will be explored, which, as we have seen, moves between fictionalization in works of art and literature to claims of idealization, distrust, and conspiracy.

A striking (and, to some, surprising) feature of freemasonry as a historical phenomenon is the rich abundance of sources, both in print and in material culture such as the use of symbolism in furniture and tools, artwork, badges, seals and insignia, as well as interior design and architecture. There is also a wealth of lavishly embellished objects for fraternal conviviality, such as plates, bowls, and glasses. As a phenomenon of well-organized sociability for 300 years, freemasonry has furthermore amassed minute books, membership lists, correspondence, economic accounts, and ritual texts for performance that have been filed in private and public archives and collections across the globe. Visitors to masonic museums, collections, and libraries such as those in London, Washington DC, Paris, or Bayreuth face the difficult task of making sense of the objects exhibited (which often reflect a male obsession with collecting and detail). Fortunately they are supported in their endeavour by a growing group of competent curators, archivists, and librarians who make an outstanding job of elucidating the subject in tours and specialized exhibitions.

The history of freemasonry is filled with names of notable lodges, grand lodges, and individual characters with their intriguing and often conflict-ridden interrelationships. Freemasonry has also produced a sizeable number of internal historical accounts, which challenge an unbiased understanding. To this literature must be added the great quantity of external treatments of freemasonry, starting with the 18th-century press and leading up to the present-day Internet, with both scholarly and sensationalist writings. Any balanced account of freemasonry has to consider this situation carefully. It is easy to get lost in the maze of fascinating yet elaborate internal history and historiography (charged with intramural significance) and lose sight of larger societal historical developments.

Freemasonry—a short overview

Modern freemasonry (which throughout this book will also be referred to as the 'brotherhood' or 'craft') became a global movement in the 18th century and its ideas have since created a considerable social, cultural, and political impact. Since its official inception in 1717, without any formal governing body, it spread throughout the world as a prominent feature of associational life. It became one of the largest non-governmental secular organizations. At the beginning of the 21st century, freemasonry has approximately two to three million members worldwide. Following a dispute over ideological matters in the 1870s, the masonic world is divided into two main spheres of influence: lodges adhering to the United Grand Lodge of England (UGLE, 1717/1813) and those adhering to the Grand Orient de France (GODF, 1738/72). Besides these two major masonic bodies there exists a large number of independent, self-authorized masonic lodges and masonic-like fraternal orders. Female membership is today a prevalent yet still disputed feature of freemasonry. And a wide range of other fraternal organizations such as the International Order of Good Templars were established, based on principles of freemasonry.

The historical origins of freemasonry are to be found in medieval professional craft-guilds for stonemasons, active in the construction of cathedrals, churches, and secular buildings around Europe. Modern freemasonry was modelled on the imaginative world of these guilds, with their architecture and geometry, mythology, symbols, feasts, and rituals, and it represents both in real and in imagined terms a continuation of this heritage. In this sense, freemasonry preserves cultural practices otherwise only to be found in guild traditions surviving into the modern era (such as the London Livery Companies, the French 'Compagnonnage', and the German 'Wanderschaft').

The medieval heritage was merged with the scientific and associational culture of the early Enlightenment, creating an eclectic mixture of intellectual and religious traditions. This undogmatic openness contributed to cultural dynamics in the development of various masonic rites and ritual systems (for the purpose of knowledge transfer) during the subsequent centuries and across the globe. Strikingly, blended into this heterogeneous mix was the powerful idea of descent from Chivalric orders in general and the Knights Templar in particular, as well as from Greek and Roman mystery cults. Thus, a historical legacy was constructed which reflected an antiquarian impulse and a revived interest in the classical era. Openness and diversity make it impossible to identify freemasonry as a unified or even unifying phenomenon. For instance, a universal coherent masonic organization was never established; rather, freemasonry promoted the development of independent local nodes (lodges) in a loose global network with instances of regional and national organization.

The common and central feature of various masonic rites is the performance of rituals for the purpose of initiation of new members or members' promotion to higher levels ('degrees', ranging from three to thirty-three, depending on the masonic system in question), where further knowledge is transferred. The pedagogical aim of masonic rituals in a progress towards higher understanding is to enhance the moral autonomy of the modern individual, which follows an enlightened programme of 'disenchantment' and in one sense sets it apart from the Christian tradition. However, it would be misguided to interpret these practices as a mere rationalization of the Christian religious impulse in content and form, since the rituals of freemasonry are saturated with influences from other religious and spiritual sources too. Most masonic rituals have appeared in various press exposures and are available in print and digital media. Thus 'secrecy' as a practice and organizational attribute of freemasonry must rather be understood as representing an elaborate societal play of trust in the interface between opacity and transparency. Freemasonry embraces a particular politics of knowledge along these limits. There will always remain a gap between insiders and outside observers and their agreement upon any 'proper' understanding of freemasonry. This tension between practitioners' and observers' perception is not necessarily an intentional aspect of freemasonry, but it is nevertheless reinforced by the culture of secrecy surrounding it.

Masonic ceremonies are enacted according to a set script (the ritual) in a private space, the lodge, and mostly followed by a formalized dinner, sometimes also called the 'table lodge' or 'agape'. The lodge is a physical location as well as being the place for ritual work, and it is the name of the smallest organizational unit within freemasonry. Several single lodges in the same region, as a rule, form a provincial lodge; and several provincial lodges form a national masonic organization or grand lodge, sometimes extending its authority to other countries, mostly occasioned by colonialism and other international relations. Autonomous grand lodges interact with each other in a self-organized system of standardization and self-regulation.

Modern freemasonry traces its organizational origin back to an alleged constitutive meeting of four lodges in London in 1717 (which most likely never took place). By 1721, a Grand Lodge of London and Westminster was fully operational. As organizational heir to this first body, the UGLE claims the right of assessing and granting the so-called regularity of other national masonic bodies in the world. Already in its first published normative text, *The Constitutions* of 1723, the tolerant and inclusive values of freemasonry are stressed, values that were compatible with the establishment of lodges in a large variety of cultural, social, and religious settings. Fifteen years later, a famous masonic oration stated that there were no significant differences between men based on language, fashion, borders, or rank. The world was here described as one vast republic, every nation as a family within it, and every individual as a child. The author claimed it was the goal of freemasonry to bring about the unity of mankind.

This idea of a universal, all-embracing brotherhood has clear elements of cosmopolitan thought that recur throughout the history of freemasonry. A universal consciousness is also represented by the frequent use of globes in seals and symbolically important furniture of the lodges, as well as in the expression to be found in a number of rites that freemasons are 'dispersed over the face of earth and water'. Moreover, freemasonry has also been involved in a number of national liberalization and independence movements across the globe. There is an inbuilt tension between a universal ideology of brotherhood and a particular ideology of individual self-determination. And despite its cosmopolitan ethos, issues of race, religion, gender, and sexual orientation illustrate the fault-lines and limits of masonic tolerance. Even today, some grand lodges in the USA have adopted the view that membership requires heterosexual orientation. Homosexual couples have been expelled and extra-marital cohabitation between heterosexual couples has been questioned. By the same token, African-American freemasonry has not been fully accepted and a racial bias is observable in recruitment to lodges and particularly to masonic leadership.

Since the early 18th century there has been a friction between established Christian churches and freemasonry. Starting with the first papal ban in 1738 (followed by many more), the Catholic Church was most prominent in its condemnation of freemasonry, culminating in the decades before World War I. In Catholic journals and pamphlets across the world, freemasonry was identified as the enemy of the Church, contributing to secularization and dissolution of traditional values. It has to be stressed, however, that these condemnations have not prevented practising Catholics from joining masonic lodges, and in countries like Ireland freemasonry was and is particularly evident (in 2017, the Grand Lodge of Ireland counted 27,000 members).

At least since the French Revolution, freemasonry has even been accused of orchestrating radical political change. Reinforced by anti-masonic and anti-Semitic writings at the turn of the 19th and into the 20th century, European right-wing groups mainly after World War I absorbed this anti-masonic ethos into their ideological and political agendas. In Italy, Spain, Portugal, and, later, Nazi Germany as well as occupied states such as France, lodges were closed down, their property seized, and individual members persecuted (see Figure 1). Also in the Soviet Union and China and in the communist regimes of central, eastern, and south-eastern Europe, freemasonry was prohibited. Cuba was and is a remarkable exception to this rule. Freemasonry and similar fraternal organizations feature today in a large variety of globally spread conspiracy theories, popularized by a vast number of Internet sites and references in popular culture. The narrative of conspiracy purports to explain everything about historical developments and current events; it is this global scope that provides the best evidence for its mania. After a negative trend in membership recruitment following the 1960s, there have been signs of recuperation not least occasioned by the collapse of Soviet communism after 1990, and many new national grand lodges have been established in central and eastern Europe.

Terminology

When it comes to terminology, the reader might already have observed that I prefer to spell 'freemasonry' ('masonic' and 'lodge') with a small initial letter. This runs contrary to conventional usage in dictionaries and I have tried to avoid confusions resulting from this choice of spelling. The reason is quite simple: freemasonry is not a unified or unifying phenomenon in history, and it appears in many different and heterogeneous varieties. No one owns the ultimate definition of its meaning. Although modern freemasonry now includes female lodges, throughout most of its history, the fraternity has been predominantly male. For this reason, I will refer to freemasons as male, with the understanding that until the last century, there were few exceptions to this rule.

Chapter 2
Three centuries of freemasonry

The organizational history of freemasonry is complex, moving between internal masonic and external non-masonic events and developments. This chapter will explore each century in detail, and while the aim is to cover global aspects of the development of freemasonry, the major focus will be on the Western hemisphere. This largely reflects the fact that the history of freemasonry in Africa and Asia is still under-researched.

The 18th century

Modern freemasonry emerged as a specialized form of voluntary and self-organized sociability within the associational world of urban London during the late 1710s. This was the time of coffeehouses, clubs, and pubs, when a nascent public sphere and press facilitated encounters between likeminded people with shared interests. Founded on previous traditions of medieval stonemasons, modern freemasonry evolved its spiritual message, rituals, and organizational forms to fit the new age of Enlightenment and scientific culture (see Figure 2). From Britain, freemasonry during the 1720s and 1730s spread successfully to the continent and the colonies, despite (or possibly because of) repeated prohibitions and a steady stream of printed so-called exposures and apologies (defences). Although the first or Premier Grand Lodge of London and Westminster (allegedly founded in 1717) assumed the role of a

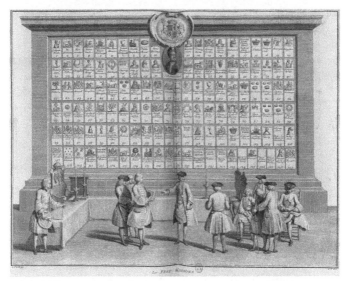

**2. Bernard Picart, 'Les Armoiries des différentes loges de Free-Massons'
(1736).**

superior body, its authority was constantly challenged within and
outside Britain by rival grand lodges.

The cultural impact of freemasonry during the first half of the
18th century was mainly confined to its recurrence as a topic in
the periodical press and in urban entertainment such as theatre
and music. During the later part of the century, the influence was
more profound, for instance in architecture, art, and literature,
particularly in a generation of German writers such as Lessing,
Goethe, and Herder. The iconic peak of masonic influence was
reached with Schikaneder's and Mozart's *The Magic Flute*
(1791), which features subjects and themes clearly related to the
imaginative world of freemasonry and other initiatory societies.

By the middle of the 18th century, masonic lodges and other orders
and fraternities were organized according to the masonic pattern

that could be found in almost every European country and were being adapted to fit diverging socio-cultural settings. Initially it was an elite phenomenon, with huge parts of the bourgeoisie increasingly embracing the masonic lodge as a prototype of enlightened sociability. It was a well-known phenomenon in the European press from the 1730s (and from the 1710s in the London press). By the 1780s the number of freemasons throughout Europe had reached at least 100,000. During the 1740s we find the first instances of female membership in separate or mixed gender lodges and orders. Female freemasonry was, however, not officially endorsed until the 1770s.

New ideas such as 'Templar imagination' contributed to the development of separate masonic degree systems (for the purpose of initiation and communication of knowledge) or 'rites'. Furthermore, a plethora of masonic-like organizations flourished, commonly described as 'secret societies'. France and the old German Empire spearheaded this dynamic between 1760 and 1790, where masonic ideas also started to influence late Enlightenment literature, art, and music. But it was also the time of dramatic political change and the potential masonic influence on the revolutions of the North American colonies (1776) and France (1789) was, and is still, a matter of debate.

Contacts between significant US and French freemasons did take place. Values as expressed in the Declaration of Independence and the US Constitution, of freedom, equality, and brotherhood, or in the French Universal Declaration of Human Rights resonated well with masonic ideas circulating at the time. On the other hand, freemasons generally displayed loyal attitudes to their respective governments, belonged to their functional elites, and were more engaged in reform than revolution. In France, freemasonry was also associated with the 'Ancien Régime' of monarchy and aristocracy and declined considerably in the aftermath of the Revolution.

Another complex issue related to the concepts circulating within freemasonry is its association with perceived core Enlightenment values such as reason, rationality, self-improvement, or the idea of progress. The perception prevails in scholarship that freemasonry was a radical and entirely secular force, a precursor of civil society preparing for change in the spirit of exoteric enlightenment aiming at a profound transformation of society. But on the other hand we find plenty of instances where freemasonry (individual or groups of freemasons) performed and engaged in more esoteric practices, such as alchemical symbolism, mesmerism, or chivalric imagination. It is not easy to find an ultimate explanation for this tension other than that it mirrors the complexity of freemasonry and the members engaged in it, which ultimately forces us to grasp the contradictory nature of Enlightenment culture and thus of modernity itself.

After the French Revolution, freemasonry faced a serious crisis throughout Europe since it was accused of undermining the 'old order' of Monarchy and Church, which resulted in a steady stream of accusatory pamphlets and books, usually seen as the starting point for the modern conspiratorial or paranoid genre.

Particularly in Catholic countries such as Austria, freemasonry experienced grave difficulties, a trend that prevailed throughout the subsequent centuries. But also in Prussia (1798) and Britain (1799), freemasonry was placed under governmental regulation. It was a period when the West saw the formation of a more mature political culture and when modern political philosophies of conservatism, liberalism, and socialism emerged. Governments started to view all political self-organization and proto-democratic activism among their citizens with increasing suspicion.

The 19th century

At the turn of the new century, Napoleon revived freemasonry in France and aligned the brotherhood closely with the ruling establishment. Thus he created the ideological basis of, and forged an elite in service to, the universalist (and expansive) project of the French Republic and later Empire. This patriotic enthusiasm, where humanist values of the Enlightenment were married with ideas of national independence and self-assertion, spilled over into a number of typically mid- and late-19th-century national freemasonries such as those in Italy, Bulgaria, or Belgium, thus influencing 'independencia' movements as far as Cuba, Mexico, and Venezuela. Within this new masonic momentum it is also possible to see a larger tolerance towards female participation in freemasonry: new mixed gender and female lodges were established. In a spirit of progress, opposition to Church and Crown, where 'traditional values' were conserved, hardened throughout the century. It caused and cemented the profound disruption between anti-clerical/secular freemasonry (predominantly in southern Europe) and Catholicism in which paranoid persecution and conspiracy theories prevailed. Between 1821 and 1884 these theories were manifested in no less than six papal constitutions and encyclicals as well as in organized Catholic anti-masonry messages across the globe. In Russia, freemasonry was eventually prohibited in 1822.

The legacy of freemasonry was also questioned in the USA. After successful foundations of grand lodges in various states, the so-called 'Morgan Affair' in 1826 led to the establishment of an anti-masonic party, the first 'third-party' political force in the USA. William Morgan, a freemason himself, had announced the publication of an exposure of masonic ritual but he disappeared subsequently under unclear circumstances. Allegedly, he was abducted by freemasons and drowned in the Niagara River. The event sparked off religious resentment (in this case from what we would today call 'evangelical' congregations) and political unrest directed against societal elites and their masonic membership. Only by the middle of the century did freemasonry in the USA recover from being persecuted. It was boosted in connection with European mass migration, particularly after the Civil War. Masonic lodges acted as contact nodes for immigrant communities, provided a link between established elites and immigrants, and occupied proto-governmental functions during Western expansion. This development continued well into the 20th century.

During the same period, freemasonries in predominantly Protestant countries such as Great Britain, Prussia, the Netherlands, Sweden, and Denmark formulated patriotic and masculine ideologies around a (theologically underpinned) monarchy in frequent personal union with the position of grand master. Masonic philanthropy (at times proactively addressing pressing social issues) was exercised *for* the people but was not in need of approval *by* the people. Generally speaking, progressive ideas of societal change and democracy in these societies drifted away to liberal factions of the bourgeoisie. These would typically choose different forms of sociability instead of freemasonry and would engage with the liberal press and nascent party politics to express their opinions.

The 19th century marks the rise of modern forms of (mass) association, from the soccer team to the trade union, pointing to significant changes in leisure, economy, and political organization. It is possible to observe an overlap between the organizational forms of freemasonry, early trade unions, and the so-called friendly societies, aiming to provide mutual help, education, social security, or to promote soberness and prohibition. This is particularly the case with Australia and its concept of 'mateship', denoting equality, loyalty, and friendship. At the end of the 19th century, new forms of fraternal orders such as the International Order of Good Templars (1851) were transferred from the USA to Europe.

A significant difference between freemasonry and the liberal bourgeoisie in Europe is the issue of nationalism. In principle a cosmopolitan movement with a universal ethos, freemasonry promoted loyalty and patriotism, but was far from adopting a national ideology based on the idea of mutually exclusive cultures. The political unification of Italy and Germany was not headed by freemasonry, although individual freemasons and masonic-like organizations such as the Italian Carbonari or the Deutsche Bund played a crucial role. As a rule, freemasonry kept its distance from emergent mass society and popular culture. Its main function at this time was to transfer the culture of the 18th-century privileged elites to the wealthy middle and upper classes of the 19th, nostalgically looking back rather than ahead towards the future. This cultural elitism prepared the ground for attacks on freemasonry by modern totalitarian ideologies of the 20th century. For them, there was no room for independent elites between leaders and their masses.

In Britain, the year 1813 marks an important event in masonic history since it was then that the two rival grand lodges of the 'Moderns' (1717) and 'Antients' (1751) merged to form the still-existing UGLE, thus creating a uniformity in practice. However, as far as the British Empire is concerned, freemasonry occupied an ambiguous role. Although in essence royalist and loyalist, the division of British freemasonry into three distinct bodies, Irish, Scottish and English, opened up different trajectories in national imagination and the projection of class-consciousness. Whereas recruitment in Ireland and Scotland and dependent lodges was more socially diversified, English lodges retained a more aristocratic and upper-class character. Andrew Prescott, a British scholar of freemasonry, has claimed that an ensuing loyalty to the monarchy engulfed British freemasonry until long after the Napoleonic wars, throwing a shadow over the fraternity for centuries to come. It has also been argued that British freemasonry promoted lay religiosity rather than secularization, and adopted well-known Anglican forms of religious ceremonies such as sermons, hymns, and prayers. In the late 19th century, freemasonry in Britain reached its Victorian peak, possibly influencing public perception well into the 1960s. As a sign of growing respectability, many purpose-built masonic halls were constructed in city centres adjacent to city halls and other public buildings. This trend can also be observed throughout the century in the USA, Germany, and the Nordic countries.

During the struggle for American independence, freemasonry did not cement political unity but rather it promoted plurality. However, according to American scholar Jessica Harland-Jacobs, British freemasonry elsewhere in later centuries tended to act as a 'builder of the Empire', consolidating British rule across the globe. At the end of the 19th century, Rudyard Kipling and his writings can be seen as representative of the inclusiveness of freemasonry in the Empire. Kipling joined the freemasons in India during the 1880s and his lodge gathered members of at least four religious creeds, which were glorified in his poem 'The Mother Lodge' (as well as in others). His novel *The Man who would be King* (1888, 1975 adapted into a feature film) has many references to freemasonry. Nonetheless, it is possible to argue that the breakaway of British lodges and the formation of 'national' and independent provincial grand lodges in the white settler colonies, such as in Canada, South Africa, and Australia, as a rule preceded their political independence.

This holds true for Norway and the unification of Switzerland as a federal state. The grand lodge Alpina (1844) was founded four years before the Swiss Confederation (1848), Den Norske Frimurerorden was granted independence from Sweden in 1891, fourteen years before the dissolution of the Swedish–Norwegian political union (ironically negotiated in a masonic hall). Freemasonry in the Middle East, an intriguing subject that only fairly recently has received appropriate scholarly attention, has mainly been interpreted as a tool of Western colonial penetration. However, it is also possible to prove a link between masonic sociability and the first Pan-Arab 'nahda', the period of cultural re-awakening combined with modernization. For instance, Abdelkader El Djezairi, an Algerian religious and military leader fighting for independence from French rule, was initiated into a French lodge. Recent scholarship has demonstrated that Arab elites handled the activities of competing European and US grand lodges in the Middle East with great self-confidence. Overcoming religious and sectarian divides, freemasons in Arab countries promoted local and regional identities and thus prepared the ground for future political independence. The same function was performed by freemasonry in Iran during the constitutional revolution of 1905–11.

Industrialization and growing social mobility created increasing pressure for substantial political reforms that could not be delivered by the conservative and reactionary Restoration regimes in Europe. The tension between bourgeois emancipation and the conservation of old privileges among the ruling elites was represented in a series of conflicts and by the 1840s culminated in various revolutions. Freemasonry was also affected by these developments. The establishment of the periodical *Freemasons' Quarterly Review* in 1834 in Britain shows how tensions relating to the role of freemasonry in society also affected its country of origin. The journal promoted a more socially active form of compassionate solidarity based firmly on Christian values, which ran contrary to the intentions of the UGLE leadership, which aimed to open up freemasonry to a larger religious diversity.

In Germany, lodges in the port city of Hamburg, one of the country's most important economic hubs at the time, pursued reforms aimed at a modernization of ritual and organizational masonic education as well as pushing for what could be called a more extroverted societal activism. This masonic reform movement spread all over Germany (and later into Switzerland and Austria too) and propagated its ideas in the masonic press. The reform movement also pushed for greater tolerance towards Jewish membership, which caused a split between more secularized forms of freemasonry and more traditional and Christian ones, such as the Prussian grand lodges. This dispute was even transferred to the USA. When German emigrés of the failed 1848 revolution (the so called '48-ers') arrived in New York and established lodges, their forthright criticisms of racial and social divides in US society immediately set them at odds with the American grand lodges. The conflict over racial issues in US grand lodges has prevailed to this day.

The split between more outspokenly political and liberal and more moderate forms of freemasonry later manifested itself on a grand European, even global, scale and has led to the erection of what Andrew Prescott has called the 'masonic equivalent of the Berlin Wall'. In 1877, the French GODF introduced the concept of a liberty of conscience concerning the masonic obligation or oath taken by each new member. Previous generations of freemasons made reference to a God of Creation (in general distinctively Christian or Abrahamic), a supreme being, as the 'Great Architect of the Universe'. This was now left to each member to decide, opening up the possibility that even atheists could join freemasonry, which ran contrary to the *Charges* of freemasonry of 1723. For the UGLE and many other grand lodges in Europe and the USA, a red line was crossed and relationships with the French GODF suspended. However, many other grand lodges followed in the French footsteps and the division in freemasonry over the issue of freedom of conscience and secularity was (and still is) a palpable reality.

The involvement of French freemasons in the short-lived Second Republic (1848–51), the later Paris Commune, and the subsequent Third Republic (1870–1940) points to two different conceptions of engaging with society that evolved during the 19th century. In Anglo-Saxon understanding, voluntary association has no political role to play by itself but is at the core of a liberal concept of self-organized (civil) society. In a more radical, continental reading, freemasonry was identified as a driving force of critical and progressive social change, possibly even social engineering. This is why we witness two ideal types of direction, already evident during the 18th century: one is introverted and 'esoteric', resistant to revolutionary ideas and existing in a state of balance with the ideological and political powers of Church and State. For these, philanthropy primarily occupies a merely charitable function. The other direction is pushing proactively for an extroverted or 'exoteric' realization of philanthropic ideas in conscious conflict with existing power relationships.

On an individual level both directions are about empowerment and thus are liberal in essence, but in different ways. The first, 'esoteric', direction places ethical responsibility upon the individual. It stresses that the role (if any) of freemasonry in society is generated by its positive influence over each member, 'making good men better' and thus better citizens of the communities in which they live. The total sum of refined and improved actions of all individual members is what any 'masonic influence' is about. It is 'intra muros' (within the walls) that refinement takes place and outside the lodges that it is practised, but with little if any corporative support of freemasonry as an organization. The 'exoteric' direction holds the individual responsible for changing society and actively intervening in the state of current affairs. Political virtues cultivated within freemasonry thus by definition necessitate socio-political action 'extra muros' (outside the walls). In this case, freemasonry as an organization aims to play a visible and formal function as an interest group in society.

However, it is not possible to maintain this clear-cut distinction in all decades of the 19th century and thereafter, and there are many overlaps. It does not hold true for all individuals who were aligned with either the one or the other direction of freemasonry. But it facilitates our understanding of the divergent standing and design of freemasonry in different political cultures. It also helps us to understand why the alleged interference of freemasonry with politics turned into a feature of violent anti-masonic feeling during the 20th century.

Significant new dynamics were brought into freemasonry through the distinct fin-de-siècle preference for mysticism. Pioneered by writers like the romanticist and early surrealist Gérard de Nerval, a more esoteric reading of freemasonry was disseminated in Europe, which was picked up by the theosophical and later anthroposophic movements. Annie Besant, British socialist, theosophist, writer, and women's rights campaigner, in 1902 established a branch of the French mixed gender grand lodge, Le Droit Humain (1893), in Britain. Le Droit Humain (DH) has today around 40,000 members worldwide. Female initiation and membership in masonic lodges occurred across Europe at the end of the 19th century, mostly as an outcome of first-wave feminism. The response of established masonic grand lodges has, however, remained divided over this issue.

The 20th century

The 20th century was characterized by a spiralling chain of international conflicts of hitherto unknown proportions and a process of radical societal modernization. At the outset of the 20th century, freemasonry had transformed from its original and dynamic 18th-century global network character to an integrated phenomenon of elite sociability confined within individual national states and empires. Masonic universalism of the earlier period had changed into diverging and mutually exclusive national definitions of what constituted universal civilization. The British, French, and German empires all competed for their specific versions of world culture. Triggered by the growing international spirit promoted by world exhibitions and the Olympic movement, by the end of the 19th century attempts had been made to create some form of universal masonic organization, an initiative that, however, in the long run remained unsuccessful. The tensions that eventually led to the outbreak of World War I demonstrate that for all its fraternal ethos, freemasonry was unable to overcome ideological and power divides between European states. During the war, we find rare instances of practised brotherhood across the frontlines, such as meetings between French and German military lodges or fraternal treatment of injured and imprisoned masonic officers and soldiers. But on a larger organizational level, the differences became insurmountable. After the human disaster of World War I, a new grand lodge building of the UGLE was erected as a masonic peace memorial in Great Queen Street in London.

In some countries that had gained political independence after the war (such as Finland), freemasonry was restored. The internal schism within freemasonry was cemented by the 1929 UGLE publication of rules for recognition that excluded a sizeable number of grand lodges from regular communications. In Germany, the defeat and the humiliating conditions of the Versailles treaty revived conspiracy myths about freemasonry that had been circulating since the end of the 19th century. During the 1920s, these were merged with the ideology of national socialism. This view of freemasonry was also prevalent in fascist ideologies and regimes of Spain, Portugal, Italy, or Serbia. But at the same time, Soviet state communism outlawed freemasonry, condemning it as a tool of bourgeois politics. Exile lodges were established in France, England, and the USA. It is no surprise that modern political totalitarian systems were incompatible with the idea of a self-organized global brotherhood.

Ultimately, the German grand lodges had sought to reconcile themselves with the Nazi regime but had failed miserably. Between 1933 and 1935, masonic lodges were closed down and their property seized, while individual freemasons faced persecution, though frequently because of other factors than their masonic membership. The Nazi obsession with eradicating freemasonry expressed itself also through a quasi-scientific treatment of the lodges and the organization of anti-masonic exhibitions, where seized objects were sensationally exposed to curious crowds. In Franco's Spain, the Falange violently suppressed freemasonry. Franco himself wrote anonymous tracts accusing freemasonry and communism of undermining the Spanish nation; in Salamanca, a lodge was transformed to a public anti-masonic exhibition centre.

As soon as World War II commenced it was clear that the fascist anti-masonry of Nazi politics would be played out in the occupied countries starting with France and the Channel Islands, where lodges were closed down and property seized or destroyed.

The actions against freemasonry were coordinated by the infamous security service, Reichssicherheitshauptamt (RSHA) in Berlin. One division of it was concerned with research into five ideological enemies: freemasonry, Jewry, political churches, Marxism, and liberalism. Seized and looted documents, libraries, and objects were recorded and analysed in order to gather proof for the alleged Judeo-masonic plot. In France this work was headed by the anti-masonic service 'Service des Sociétés Secrètes' under the Vichy government, which prepared card indexes of freemasons who were believed to pose a danger to the regime. Hundreds of freemasons were sent to prison. Manuscripts and prints from looted masonic lodges were also amassed for further analysis in the national library in Paris and an anti-masonic exhibition was organized as early as 1940, which shows the importance given to freemasonry.

Interestingly, the Soviet secret service later looted the masonic collections that had been transported to the RSHA in Berlin a second time, which is why large numbers of collections, particularly from the occupied countries, ended up in Moscow. Apart from Britain and Ireland (with the exception of the Channel Islands), only the grand lodges of Sweden and Switzerland were not affected by fascist or communist persecution in Europe during World War II, and in Finland the situation of freemasonry was highly contested.

After the war, freemasonry continued to be prohibited in the countries of the Eastern Bloc. However there are signs that some unofficial masonic activity was going on even in socialist countries. The great turn occurred with the collapse of the Iron Curtain after 1990, when new grand lodges were established in the countries of central and eastern Europe and old grand lodges were revived. Whereas GODF and other grand lodges in France restored their activities relatively quickly after World War II and still today exercise a considerable activity and impact in French culture and society (170,000 members), the situation in divided Germany was far more complex. The existence of American, British, and Canadian freemasonry among the allied occupation forces led to the establishment of two grand lodges which together with the other West German grand lodges formed an umbrella organization. Whereas freemasonry in Germany before Nazi prohibition counted between 60,000 and 80,000 members, the figure has shrunk to around 16,000 today. This has to be compared with Denmark (where freemasonry also was suppressed during the war), which currently has around 10,000 members, despite the country being sixteen times smaller in population. German re-unification has not led to any significant increase in total membership. After almost seventy years of ideological persecution, East Germany has been without active freemasons for two generations and there is no living memory or tradition to continue.

It has yet to be established precisely when and how anti masonry entered the Arab world, and was integrated into anti-Israeli and anti-Western world conspiracy and victim myths. During the late 19th and early 20th century, freemasonry was not incompatible with Arab culture or Pan-Arab nationalism. However, in its 1988 charter, Hamas branded freemasonry a 'Zionist' organization and militant Jihadism has generally adopted this view.

As the Canadian scholar of freemasonry J. Scott Kenney has argued, growth of American freemasonry during the first half of the century was aided by the organization of social services and insurance practices when public social programmes were virtually non-existent. During what has been called 'the golden age of fraternalism', a host of spinoff organizations or so-called 'concordant bodies' (such as the Shriners) were founded. American freemasonry changed its character in the middle of the century, when big business, government, as well as labour organizations increasingly influenced socio-economic development.

Service clubs like the Rotary (1905) and Lions (1917) attracted more and more members and served social needs in more modernized work-life patterns. Previously, ritual and self-improvement constituted the main focus of the American lodges, but new times occasioned a shift towards high levels of organization, institutionalization, and bureaucracy in the management of various relatively large-scale philanthropies. Masonic membership peaked in the decades following World War II, but like many other community organizations it has experienced a significant decline since the 1960s. Despite many efforts and programmes to recruit new and retain old members, the overall figure has continued to drop.

There are several explanations for this trend; first of all, the gradual substitution of freemasonry's social service and insurance functions. Secondly, sociologist Robert Putnam claims that traditional social capital in America has increasingly been undermined in the post-war era. In the course of rapid modernization it was replaced by other patterns of leisure organization and gender roles to which freemasonry with its essentially male character was unable to respond. Thirdly, a long period of relative prosperity fostered a culture of self-satisfaction and indifference among the middle classes, where the membership of a community organization was no longer perceived as attractive. Rumours, prejudices, and the occasional scandals associated with freemasonry, which had been quickly disseminated in an age of social media, further deter people from getting involved.

In Britain, it has been suggested that the decline of freemasonry can be linked with the secularization of society as a whole: the Victorian and Anglican character of freemasonry with its quasi-religious undertones would explain a certain amount of the disaffection. On the other hand, it was precisely from religious groups (the Methodists and the United Reformed Church) that attacks on freemasonry were launched during the 1980s and its compatibility with Christianity questioned, as it was in evangelical movements across the globe to the present day. Heavy criticism of British freemasonry, with such publications as *The Brotherhood* (1983) and

Inside the Brotherhood (1989), was left unchallenged, leaving the field open to accusations and allegations that ultimately resulted in two official parliamentary investigations into the role of freemasonry in public life (between 1997 and 1999). Within a period of two decades, British public perception and governmental treatment of freemasonry resembled the situation immediately after the French Revolution. A similar development occurred in the Nordic countries at the end of the 1990s when a Norwegian historian of religion published an exposure of the secretive Swedish rite. When the story broke in the evening press, masonic organizations found themselves perplexed and lacking in credible media strategies to respond to the external pressure. By the 1990s freemasonry was characterized by heavy bureaucratization, over-institutionalization, and an ageing and declining membership. It was unable to counter the increasing amount of negative press in the new digital age and its demands for immediate transparency.

The 21st century

It is always challenging to reflect on and interpret contemporary events, but it is possible to account for a few lines of development that have characterized the first fifteen or so years of the new millennium. First of all, research into freemasonry has increased to a new level through academic and masonic collaboration. Political developments after 1990 made huge amounts of source material looted by the Nazis (and then again by the Soviets) available, in some cases dating back more than 250 years to when they were originally kept as the private property of individual lodges. While these records were subsequently returned to their original owners, collections frequently ended up in public archives, open to non-masonic researchers given certain restrictions. This happened, for instance, in Germany, simply for pragmatic reasons: most lodges had been eradicated and their buildings destroyed between 1935 and 1945.

A new availability of sources prompted private masonic collections also to adopt a more open policy. Pioneered by individual researchers during the last decades of the 20th century, a new generation of academics turned to sources that had never been consulted before. Furthermore, around the year 2000, the UGLE and the Dutch Order of Freemasons invested in university-based research initiatives (in Sheffield and Leiden), an example which has been followed by the Grand Lodges of California and of Canada (Ontario) and other masonic initiatives. Platforms for international congresses were established, bringing together academics and freemasons who share common research interests.

These joint ventures have however not proven to be without friction since the internal perspectives of practitioners in freemasonry frequently clash with the external, problematizing, and critical analyses of their observers. This holds particularly true when masonic issues such as the divide between different forms of freemasonry, the alleged role of freemasonry in important historical developments, or female freemasonry are addressed. Common understanding has yet to be established. Within academia, PhD and research projects have been carried out and a string of conferences and symposia have been arranged. All these initiatives have in sum created a huge body of academic literature and new insights into the historical development of freemasonry, with its cultural and social implications. New light has for instance been shed on freemasonry in the Middle East, female participation, freemasonry as a topic in the 18th-century press, or its significance as a rare instance of esoteric practices in a Western context. This trend towards more quality-assessed research contributes to a larger transparency. Within freemasonry, public relations processes have also been adapted to the digital age in which social media and Internet presence are self-evident tools for communication and interaction with members as much as with the society in which they exist.

A second trend, however contradictory, is that despite the open availability of academically assessed research and transparent information politics from most grand lodges, misapprehensions, negative stereotypes, and conspiracy myths do still prevail. They exercise a considerable and persistent influence upon popular perception, media, and culture, a trend that has only accelerated in the digital age. Tens of thousands of search results on the Internet will tell its readers about plots of world dominance, the 'true' meaning of the One Dollar note, or that pop stars and actors use their music and movies to disseminate masonic or alleged 'Illuminati' symbols in order to control the mind-set of the masses. Claims are made that communists, capitalists, Zionists, aliens, the Bilderberg Group, Jesuits, the CIA, and the mafia alike all use freemasonry or other secret societies as a smoke-screen for their evil machinations, working to bring about the collapse of human society as we know it. The problematic side of this development is that the age of the Internet has also created phenomena like fact-resistant echo chambers where people only listen to information that confirms whatever they want to hear.

Partly, this development has been championed by a new wave of fiction about freemasonry promoted in books like Dan Brown's *The Da Vinci Code* (2003) or *The Lost Symbol* (2009; explicitly referencing freemasonry) or movies like *National Treasure* (2004). These fictional accounts meet popular demand for narratives in which world history really is structured by a band of conspirators who are invisible to the general public. Possibly this is a reaction to secularization and the alleged disappearance of master narratives in our late or post-modern world. When sense no longer is provided coherently by institutions or authorities like Church, science, literature, or education, people are inclined to search for meaning elsewhere.

The third trend refers to a contemporary resurgence of interest in masonic membership. This might be occasioned by the impact of popular culture, the new openness in masonic public relations, or a new willingness to engage in community organizations on a local level. Another reason might be that the uncertainties of the late modern world make membership in a centuries-old organization attractive. It promises to connect back in time and provide space for traditional and offline forms of ritualized and quite elaborate (usually male) sociability with direct interpersonal encounters. Indeed, as discussed earlier, recent years have witnessed a growing female participation in freemasonry. Despite these trends, divisive issues of religion, race, gender, and sexual orientation do still haunt freemasonry on a global level. Meanwhile, the threat remains that a resurgence of authoritarian politics worldwide might once again negatively impact upon the brotherhood.

Chapter 3
Historical legacies

There is no coherent ideology or doctrine of freemasonry.
Rather, the fraternity is characterized by a considerable
conceptual inclusiveness promoting an ethics of action; that
is, an ethics of application rather than theory. Another joint
feature of the ideas in freemasonry is that they all aim to
promote processes of real and imagined community building,
establishing bonds between individuals, and across nations and
epochs historically. Throughout the centuries, freemasonry has
absorbed concepts of the past as much as those of its present
age. Thus a unique eclectic mix has been established that
embraces central ingredients of Western thought and appears
in multiple layers. Ideas in freemasonry are mainly manifested
through the live performance of ritual and a specific visual
culture whereby ideas are expressed through symbols, emblems,
and interior design. The idea of the secret and of secrecy is of
paramount importance in freemasonry, both as an organizing
principle and in the transfer of knowledge. Over the centuries,
masonic ideas have also been set out in writing—in books,
orations, and songs as well as in an abundance of sources
in the periodical press.

The first of these layers of ideas has a strong medieval connection
in two peculiar regards, one imagined and one real. Modern
freemasonry inherited its organizational structures, symbols, and

mythologies from medieval craft guilds, tying it directly to the unified and holistic worldview of the Middle Ages. This worldview is essentially Christian in character, meaning that human or secular events and actions are placed within a divine or sacred framework of explanations which are represented as being the outcome of 'intelligent design' (see Figure 3). Apart from this strongly religious commitment, which particularly influenced the master builders of European cathedrals, medieval craft guilds composed their own mythological histories. The master topic of masonic mythology was the Temple of Solomon in the Old Testament, since it provided a sacred biblical reference to the building profession.

3. God as the architect of the world (1400s).

The second medieval connection was constructed in retrospect during the 18th century, and comprised a presumed link to the orders of knighthood in general and to the Knights Templar (disbanded in 1307–14) in particular. This imagined genealogy has proved to be extremely powerful within freemasonry and has indeed fired the imagination of external viewers. The idea that freemasonry represents a continuation of medieval knighthood can be understood on several levels: as a playground for fanciful imagination, as a sign that Enlightenment elites feared loss of social status, or as the development of a new utopian and self-conscious elitism in opposition to those of Crown and Church.

However, the question of how far freemasonry represents or ought to represent explicit Christian references was and still is a matter of debate, since professing to belong to a particular denomination would collide with the universal, tolerant, and inclusive ethos of the fraternity. When it comes to religion, three directions developed during the past few centuries, in principle. Some grand lodges and rites require a confession of Christian faith, some require belief in an unspecified supreme being (and hence some form of religious confession), and some do not ask their members for any specific belief (leaving the matter of belief in a supreme being or god entirely to the individual conscience). To these general positions, it must be added that at the turn of the 19th century, freemasonry developed a considerable interest in theosophy and pagan religious traditions, not least inspired by a surge of interest in Egyptian and Indian religions.

During the Renaissance, the unified worldview of the Middle Ages was slowly replaced with a new appreciation of Europe's classical past, bringing back Greek and Roman philosophy to form the core of intellectual culture in general, and of the arts and aesthetics in particular. The Renaissance also opened up an appreciation for what we would today call 'esoteric' practices; making them an integrated part of a general culture of knowledge rather than keeping them separate from what modernity defined as pure sciences.

Guild traditions

The different guilds of craftsmen across medieval Europe all sought to promote their own significance by developing a craft mythology, linking their particular trade and skills to biblical references and the legends of Christian patron saints. Both St Johns are traditionally associated with the craft of masonry; the day of St John the Baptist is June 24th and that of St John the Evangelist is December 27th, which explains why the summer and winter solstices played an important role in the gatherings and festivities of medieval masons.

As with so many issues of rank, the aspect of age was decisive—the more ancient the roots and prominent (sacred and secular) the patronage a craft could claim, the higher its status among other guilds, and the greater capacity it had to mobilize political power. The guilds filled an important function in the medieval city: they regulated professional life, wages, and prices; they participated in political representation and security for the town; they provided education and social security to their members (including widows and orphans); and they occupied an important function as lay fraternities, engaged in religious festivities such as mystery plays or processions. This religious role was almost erased in Protestant Europe after the Reformation. The modern state (together with its new economic theories) was not interested in guild privileges and internally agreed trade monopolies. More and more of the traditional functions of guilds were taken over by public authorities, and more and more trade privileges were abandoned. It has also been argued that the capitalist economy had a powerful impact in superseding the self-regulated 'moral economy' of the guilds.

Originally, the regulations for craft masonry were firmly based within the imaginative world of medieval Christian religion. These regulations also reflected how religion was used in the construction of a mythical historical past, which played an important symbolic function in the self-fashioning of medieval craft guilds and their role in urban lay religiosity. Similarly, history could be mobilized in the negotiation of power relationships within the medieval city and with the feudal hierarchy in general. It would be wrong to require historical accuracy in these accounts, since they were not primarily written to provide objective descriptions of the past, but rather to claim legacy and prestige. For example, it was not until the Renaissance that it was revealed that the 'Donation of Constantine'—an 8th-century manuscript purporting to describe the surrender of secular power by the Roman emperor to the pope—was in fact a forgery.

Another important feature of medieval craft guilds was that, in a time of widespread illiteracy and an absence of printed books, practical and applied know-how was orally transmitted and treated as privileged insider knowledge, constituting the secrets of a trade. Medieval society was organized into strict hierarchies and thus knowledge within the guilds was transferred vertically from master to journeyman to apprentice. The craft guild was a professional, social, and religious fraternity, as well as representing a community of knowledge. To be admitted into such a community marked a significant transition, and the acquisition of further knowledge implied authority, responsibility, status, and access to privileges both within the trade and within society. Many guilds developed special ceremonies and customs to mark these different transitions, unquestionably inspired by similar practices in the clergy, at universities, and in the knighthood.

Masonry occupied a particular position in medieval society at that time since it involved active work with geometry, the fifth of the so-called 'Seven Liberal Arts' (grammar, dialectic, rhetoric, arithmetic, geometry, astronomy, and music) that dominated the medieval understanding of science. The term 'freemason' refers to a mason who specializes in carving freestone (sandstone or limestone) for the decoration of capitals and cornices. The ability to apply the laws of geometry in the construction of cathedrals and major secular buildings exhibited a person's possession of attractive and superior knowledge.

As the medieval historian Andrew Prescott has pointed out, in the British context, freemasonry originates, as a social movement, in the religious fraternities of the 14th century, which, following the devastating societal impact of the Black Death, increasingly took over the responsibilities of trade regulation. Most medieval craft ordinances are concerned with practical issues of guild organization. The first known manuscript outlining the legends of freemasonry dates from around 1425 and is preserved to this day in two versions (the Regius and the Cooke manuscripts). The main claims of these legends are that masons were provided with ancient charters allowing them to hold assemblies and that all masons were brethren of equal status. As in many pre-modern conflicts, the masons (as an association of craftsmen) sought to protect their privileges (including level of payment) and independence by referring to their seniority and noble protection (provided by a fictitious Anglo-Saxon prince). The same pattern was repeated a century and a half later when inflation threatened to lower the wages of craftsmen. A new, presumed royal, protection was incorporated into the legends, specifically mentioning York. Between 1583 and 1717, more than twenty manuscripts with the 'old charges' of freemasonry were produced.

Knighthood imagined

In a widely disseminated speech delivered to French freemasons in the late 1730s (Ramsay's 'Discours'), the claim was made that freemasonry had descended from the chivalric orders of the crusades. Although this speech made a passionate case for cosmopolitan ideas and a pan-European masonic initiative to produce a joint encyclopaedia of sciences and arts, it was the link to medieval knighthood that was presented as the central inspiration of freemasonry. Around 1740, the idea started to circulate that freemasonry represented a secret continuation of the Order of the Knights Templar. The story was that, due to the suppression of the Order by the king of France and the pope between 1307 and 1314, the Knights Templar had sought refuge in Scotland where they had attached themselves to the brotherhood of masons and begun to share in their secret practices.

This story is not backed up by any reliable historical evidence whatsoever. However, by the fact or through the fact that it was told and had a strong impact, we can see more clearly how freemasonry was fashioning itself, with men belonging to the elite of society in the European Enlightenment constructing a link back to an order of knighthood from the medieval period. This apparent link sparked off a considerable explosion in masonic degrees, rituals, and motifs that continued to unfold over the subsequent five decades. The development was encouraged by a stream of publications on medieval monastic and chivalric orders, which occurred in parallel with a surge in the establishment of honours systems offering a range of knighthoods for various purposes in Europe. Between 1748 and 1772, for instance, Sweden introduced no less than four state orders of merit offering the prospect of 'knighthood' for exceptional achievements.

A leading expert in the area, Pierre Mollier, claims that the introduction of new chivalric ideas and the popularity of these ideas resulted in the creation of new legendary tales (a so-called 'legendary circle'). The epic tale of the persecution of the Knights Templar, the injustice of their Order's termination, their escape to Scotland, their alleged secret knowledge and immense wealth, their unification with the freemasons, and their plans for revenge was fleshed out with new details. Versions of the Templar legend multiplied, adding new details to the imaginary world of masonic chivalry. In organizational terms, chivalric degrees were added to the first three craft degrees, and separate masonic Orders were also established, in which the Templar legend formed the basis for the supreme hierarchy.

There are four major traditions in freemasonry. From France, the Templar motif was transported to the USA and became what is known today as the 'Ancient and Accepted Scottish Rite' (AASR) with thirty-three degrees. In Great Britain, the Knights Templar were established during the 1780s and 1790s, eventually leading to the formation of an independent fraternal order strongly affiliated to freemasonry. In the 'York Rite' (mostly practised in the Americas) Christian Knights Templar degrees are also prevalent. Starting around 1750, a number of rites developed in continental Europe, where the Knights Templar motif is still practised at higher degree levels. Most prominent in this regard was the pan-European masonic rite of 'Strict Observance' (1751–82), which sub-divided Europe into different provinces of the Order. After 1782, the chivalric heritage of the Strict Observance was transformed into the 'Scottish Rectified Rite', which had a strong theosophical dimension.

A still-existing independent tradition of Templar masonry developed in Scandinavia (with offshoots in Germany and the Baltics): the so-called 'Swedish rite'. The Swedish semi-official decoration 'Order of Charles XIII' has strong connections to Templar motifs.

It is also important to take the political context of the 18th century into account. The Jacobite Stuart monarchy was ousted from Britain at the end of the 17th century and the deposed king and his heirs were forced to live in exile in France, from where several unsuccessful attempts were launched to recapture the throne. The Hanoverian dynasty that ruled Britain from 1714 onwards was perceived as illegitimate by the Jacobites. In the masonic Templar legend, the Stuart monarchy occupied an important position; hence, it was possible to project the unjust fate of the Knights Templar upon the entire Jacobite cause, not least through the imagined nexus to Scotland. Although this sub-text to the Templar legend ceased to play any significant practical role after the failed

Jacobite uprising of 1746, the Templar myth was charged with a political dimension from that point on. In the aftermath of the French Revolution, freemasonry's imagined link with the Templars was used as proof for a presumed conspiracy against Church and Crown. Outside of freemasonry, neo-Templarism has subsequently served as a projection screen for various ideas on alternative chains of historical events, forcefully illustrated by books such as *Holy Blood, Holy Grail* (1982), a significant source of *The Da Vinci Code* (2003). The Templar motif has even inspired French surrealist tradition; writer Guillaume Apollinaire identified with their fate:

> Flamboyant Templars, I burn amongst you / together Grand Master let's prophesy I am / The desirable fire that consigns itself to you / and the Catherine wheel turns around / o lovely lovely night. (From 'The Betrothal (to Picasso)' in the poetry collection *Alcools*, 1913)

Modern freemasonry united two features of medieval culture, one real and one imagined: the historical link to the craft guilds (symbolized by the trowel) and the imagined link to chivalry (symbolized by the sword). Whereas architecture and construction could symbolize the perfect ideal of bringing peaceful change to the world, the association with the martial culture of knighthood is more complex. On the one hand, the idea of chivalry was apparently attractive to the elite of the Enlightenment, as a metaphor of refined morality. On the other hand, the question remains of what function references to the violent history of a defunct and suppressed order of knighthood could occupy. Pierre Mollier has pointed out two dimensions: first, that of the occult and myth, according to which the Knights Templar were yet another secret community in which arcane mysteries were kept and transferred; and, second, the political dimension, which calls for the restoration of justice and law. The alleged heresy of the order thus provides a link between esotericism and social protest.

Hieroglyphs, emblems, and vision: the Renaissance heritage

During the Renaissance, the medieval canon of knowledge was slowly replaced with more sophisticated scientific, aesthetic, and religious ideas, still resting firmly on a Christian basis. Cultural encounters with the Arab world, accelerated by the fall of Constantinople in 1453, brought new historical awareness, language skills, and the re-discovery of primary sources of antiquity, which were revered as examples of perfection. It was now possible to read re-constructed original texts by classical thinkers such as Plato, Aristotle, or Cicero, bringing philosophy back to a broad readership. Theologians were at pains to explain the compatibility of the European pagan past with Christianity. Further blows to the ideological authority of the Church were occasioned by the advent of the printing press, European expeditions around the globe, and the pioneering discoveries of the scientific revolution. Finally, the Reformation undermined the former unity of the medieval worldview through a conscious elimination of Catholic religion and a preference for a direct reading of the Holy Scriptures.

Under the surface of Protestantism, mystical currents of religiosity emerged, such as Rosicrucianism, which radically individualized the spiritual and personal encounter with the divine, and charged it with strong symbolism. One of the master themes of the period was the search for secret and revealed analogies and correspondences between microcosm and macrocosm, heaven and earth, visible and invisible, and divine and human. During this period, hermetic and mystical ideas such as alchemy, astrology, and Christian readings of Jewish Kabbalah were also disseminated. For freemasonry, this intellectual development meant that most of its privileged knowledge relating to geometry and architecture was available publicly in print from around 1500; that the Gothic paradigm of architecture was replaced by a new appreciation for classical examples of style; and that some features belonging to the hermetic tradition of thought found their way into masonic practices.

Essentially a revolution of vision, the Renaissance re-established and refined the rules of central perspective and three-dimensionality. Optical instruments such as the microscope and the telescope accelerated the process known as the scientific revolution with an ever-growing number of new discoveries. However, these are only the external aspects of a movement that also embraced the idea that 'seeing' and 'vision' were a divine skill exclusive to the select few who were equipped with more-or-less arcane knowledge. The radiant 'All-Seeing Eye of God' placed within a perfect triangle (a prominent symbol in freemasonry as well) became a symbol for these deeper levels of the all-seeing of visible and invisible dimensions. Both in original art and in printed artwork such as frontispieces and etchings, a veritable play of hide-and-seek developed in which hints and references to ancient pagan mythology and philosophy as well as to the Christian religion were displayed in a visual narrative. Medieval art had already developed a predefined and stereotyped system of symbolic references to saints and biblical episodes which was manifested in miracle plays and Christian typology (in which the faithful, for instance, identify with the Stations of the Cross). However, the Renaissance and subsequent periods brought these expressions to new heights, particularly disseminated through books on architecture.

In such books, hieroglyphs were understood as representing a divine and universal language that would immediately reveal their sense to the initiated viewer. Emblematic books displayed moral and philosophical images with mottos and epigrams. Pictures were used as condensed rhetorical narratives of philosophical and religious self-reflection. Freemasonry bought into this tradition and is still burdened with symbols that assume multiple layers of meaning. As three-dimensional objects, these symbols come to life in masonic ritual where they are used in the performance and contribute to the creation of ritualistic time and space. As visual symbols, they are displayed in masonic prints, on regalia and furniture, and, most significantly, on so-called tracing boards in the middle of lodge rooms. These tracing boards show the significant symbols of each degree in which they are used.

As historian David Stevenson has pointed out, 'Scotland's century' in the development of freemasonry occurred within this period. The Reformation heavily influenced all organized forms of religious and lay fraternities in Britain, including the medieval guild system. In Scotland in particular, signs of recovery can be found and, in 1598/9, new statutes of masonry were issued (the 'Schaw Statutes'). These statutes regulated the organization of Scottish masonry, establishing the practice of a double organization: on a local and broader territorial level. Stevenson argues that the re-organization of Scottish masonry at this time coincided exactly with the intellectual impact of the Renaissance. The Schaw Statutes explicitly mention the 'art of memory and science'—which might refer to the hermetic practices circulating in Europe at that time. During the 17th century, the first instances occurred of the admission of non-craftsmen to the lodges in both Scotland and England, an occurrence that might point to overlaps in intellectual interests or simply to a shared desire for refined sociability.

Chapter 4
Enlightenment foundations

When freemasonry entered the 18th century, a new layer of ideas was added: the brotherhood associated itself and was associated with science in general and with the new culture of Newtonian experimental science in particular. For the first time, masonic ideas were being published. During this first phase of its modern existence, there was considerable overlap between scientific culture and freemasonry. Lodges were perceived as something akin to academies, or at least they acted as such in countries that were without scientific societies. The scientific image of freemasonry gave it a central place in the Enlightenment ideas of the period. Freemasonry is saturated with key Enlightenment concepts such as progress, perfectibility, and cosmopolitanism. On an individual level, freemasonry aims to promote a morality of autonomy, responsibility for the self, and moral example. These ideas are heavily influenced by classical stoicism: attaining a strong control of the passions and a mastery of the emotions while facing personal fate and any unforeseen challenges. However, there is also an epicurean element, with the philosophical terms of 'felicity' and 'happiness' (derived from Greek concepts of 'Eudaimonia') occupying a prominent place in masonic ideology and symbolism, such as the omnipresent 'Temple of Felicity'.

While these ideas primarily served to refine the individual freemason's practice, the core masonic concept of 'charity' could historically be read in two ways. From the start, freemasons have raised funds and sponsored medical, educational, and cultural initiatives and institutions. In one sense, masonic charity thus anticipated central aspects of the modern welfare system, without necessarily having a particular political agenda. In another sense, it is possible to detect a growing engagement with burning social issues, particularly after 1800, in connection with industrialization and the formation of mass society. In some countries, freemasonry defined itself as a socio-political force working towards the progress of society in its entirety and not as simply focused on the moral refinement of its individual members. These two different positions related to the potential societal impact of masonic ideas in society have engaged freemasonry ever since.

The ideas of modern freemasonry: the 1723 *Constitutions*

When modern freemasonry emerged in urban London in the late 1710s, there was an apparent need to gather, print, and edit documents from earlier periods in order to make an ideological statement. This happened in 1723 with the publication of *The Constitutions of the Freemasons. Containing the History, Charges, Regulations &c. of that most Ancient and Right Worshipful Fraternity. For the Use of the Lodges*, a work of roughly 100 pages that still is considered to be the major foundational document and expression of masonic ideas (see Figure 4). Within two decades, *The Constitutions* had been translated into all major European languages. They were published again in 1738 as an amended second edition and have since been republished in innumerable versions over the last three centuries.

Engraved by John Pine in Aldersgate Street London

4. Frontispice of James Anderson, *The Constitutions of the Free-Masons* (1723).

The Constitutions demonstrate in print how the transformation of the old medieval craft organization manifested itself in the new age of Enlightenment. The tension inherent in such a transformation can be problematic to interpret. The dedication to the then grand master, the Duke of Wharton, is signed by John Theophilus Desa(u)guliers. Desaguliers was an exiled French Huguenot and a disciple of Newton who made his living through popular lectures, publications, and demonstrations of experimental science. A Scottish priest, James Anderson (1679–1739), compiled and edited *The Constitutions* from existing sources and from his own imagination. The first part, representing almost half of the book, outlines the sacred mythology of freemasonry from the biblical age to its (then) contemporary situation. The second part is devoted to 'The Charges of a Free-mason': rules and regulations for individual freemasons, lodges, and their mutual interrelationship. This second part—although it includes significant normative statements—is of a far more administrative and organizational character than the first, mythological part. To unlock its peculiar narrative, it is necessary to embrace the pre-modern logic of sacred history, in which facts and religious meaning are intermingled. The book concludes with a number of programmatic songs.

Against this background, it is even more thought provoking that the ideas behind one of the most significant medieval guilds, the stonemasons, were rescued at the outset of the Enlightenment and re-imagined in the new form of *The Constitutions*. The first part of *The Constitutions* cannot simply be dismissed as a product of pure imagination; rather, this heavily fictionalized account of history should be understood as fulfilling a function. By the same token, however, it is no wonder that a fictionalized autobiography of freemasonry would open the fraternity up for ridicule, distrust, speculation, and ideas of conspiracy.

The editor of *The Constitutions* meticulously placed freemasonry within the framework of the biblical narrative since creation. Accounts of secular history are interwoven with sacred mythology. The art of building, architecture, and geometry are all represented as exemplifying divine power and interference in human conditions exercised by the 'Great Architect of the Universe' (GAOTU). All important buildings mentioned in the Bible or known to the editor through classical literature and existent historical remains are linked to the science of masonry. Construction and re-construction are used as powerful metaphors of civilization, not as an abstract philosophy, but as an ethics of action in the service of humanity. Geometry and architecture occupy a civilizing function as expressions of divine order, providing a potential pattern 'for all nations' to follow and disseminate to distant cultures as far as Africa or India. A recurring idea expressed in Anderson's historical account is the opposition of freemasonry to war and destruction, which are represented metaphorically by 'Goths and Mahometans'. Architecture is a symbol of peace, prospering as it does in conditions of peace and freedom in 'polite Nations', especially 'when the Civil Powers, abhorring Tyranny and Slavery, gave due Scope to the bright and free Genius of their happy Subjects'.

It is striking that the biblical narrative is frequently amended with non-biblical apocryphal content, emulations, or supplements. It is unclear exactly to what extent or where in the volume Anderson as editor (and, remarkably, priest) was using old masonic manuscripts, other sources, or his own imagination. Furthermore, he blends biblical history with other mythologies and pagan religious traditions such as those of the Persian magi, Egyptian priests, and Greek schools of mystery and philosophy, such as Pythagoras and Plato. Despite this mixture of belief systems, the central leitmotif of masonic mythology is that of the Temple of Solomon: its construction, destruction, and subsequent reconstruction; and the organization of labour and personages associated with the building, such as by the master architect Hiram Abif. Anderson's major claim is that the Romans took over freemasonry from its previous practitioners and brought it to excellence under Caesar Augustus and his peaceful reign, during which Christ was born. It is Roman architecture that Anderson presents as the model for perfect proportions. Roman skills and traditions are described as being passed on until the medieval period, when they were first revived in Gothic architecture—which Anderson stigmatizes for its 'wrong' design.

It is only with the Renaissance and the recovery of the writings of Vitruvius on architecture that, according to Anderson, pure Augustan form and design were re-established. He frequently opposes the (revived) ancient Roman style with medieval architecture and refers to it as 'Gothic ignorance' or 'rubbish'. When discussing medieval history, he is diligent in quoting old English sources (real and imagined) that demonstrate the historical legacy of freemasonry. Kings of Scotland and England are shown to protect and promote the craft, and the link between monarchy and masonry is reinforced by the use of the term 'royal art' as a synonym for masonry. Scotland's privileged position in preserving freemasonry is stressed.

Anderson's mythological account of freemasonry establishes a grandiose genealogy throughout the entire spectrum of intellectual history, encompassing the secular, Christian, and pagan. Thus he constructs a narrative in which freemasonry is in possession of eternal ancient wisdom and uncorrupted knowledge of religion ('philosophia perennis' or 'prisca theologia'), handed down by generations of sage men united over the centuries and millennia in a privileged chain of initiates from almost every important religious and philosophical tradition. This kind of genealogical thinking is prevalent in European historiography until well into the 18th century and was only slowly replaced by a more scientific approach to presenting the past and demonstrating the authenticity of historical sources. When discussing modern times, Anderson stresses that freemasonry is regulated by British law and thus can claim a semi-public position in British society.

Published in the new Hanoverian era, some parts of *The Constitutions* can almost be read as a national narrative for the then fairly recently formed United Kingdom, outlining a civilizing mission and forecasting an ideology of the Empire. It is also possible to read subtle commentaries about fundamental political values between the lines, such as the relation between the rulers and the ruled, and between freedom and the right to self-organization in what we would today call civil society. Thus, for all its sacred references, *The Constitutions* can clearly be placed within a liberal tradition of political thought.

Another important aspect of *The Constitutions* is that it was actually intended for use in the oral instruction of a newly admitted member. Whether realistic or not (given the vast number of pages), such a usage would indicate that this mythological account of the history of freemasonry should be read as a piece of rhetoric; an oration that aims to pass on a vision of the fraternity as rooted in the major intellectual traditions of humankind; a concept of identity for the new age in which it was active. The narrative character of *The Constitutions* is further underlined by the fact that this mythological history was turned into a lengthy song in five parts with no less than twenty-eight verses in the final part of the publication. Another song, with fewer stanzas but roughly following the same storyline, was also added. As such, *The Constitutions* could function as a source of inspiration for the composition of rituals. Frequent reference is made to the premise that freemasonry cannot be communicated in writing, pointing to its central dimension being performance. Finally, *The Constitutions* reflects on the inbuilt tension between secrecy and transparency; between internally communicated knowledge and external perceptions (from religious and political authorities).

The part entitled 'The Charges of a Free-Mason', which follows immediately after the historical account in *The Constitutions*, includes six items: (1) 'Of God and religion'; (2) 'On the civil magistrate supreme and subordinate'; (3) 'Of lodges'; (4) 'Of masters, wardens, fellows and apprentices'; (5) 'Of the management of the Craft in working'; and (6) 'Of behaviour' (sub-divided into six different situations of behaviour, when freemasons meet internally or with strangers).

Much has been written about these charges and their presumed meaning. Suffice it to say that the first two charges proclaim a quietly liberal and tolerant attitude towards religion and politics, within certain limits. A freemason has to obey the 'moral law' and never be a 'stupid atheist' or an 'irreligious libertine'. Instead of confessing a particular religion, freemasons are obliged to hold 'to that religion in which all men agree' and to be 'good men and true' and 'men of honour and honesty'. Differences are thus overcome in favour of union, 'conciliating true friendship among persons that must have remain'd at a perpetual distance'. Without denying the existence of God or relativizing religion through plain materialism, freemasons are asked to overcome the particularity of their confessions and agree to a shared moral compromise (which receives its authority from 'nature'), visible in personal qualities rather than in abstract doctrines. This compromise is intended to create a bond of union between strangers. It is obvious that freemasonry aimed to leave behind the devastating religious conflicts of the 17th century and to establish a forward-looking compromise of reconciliation, one that was potentially open to all forms of religious confession.

The second charge commits freemasons to loyalty and to staying out of 'Plots and Conspiracies against the Peace and Welfare of the Nation' and the representatives of power. Peace is the ideal condition for freemasonry to prosper. The second part of this (second) charge has been subject to a considerable amount of debate, since it appears to require the fraternity to be tolerant of brothers who are 'Rebels against the State'. Although such behaviour is portrayed as unacceptable and wrong, rebellion alone is not seen to be adequate reason for expelling a member from the lodge. It appears that modern freemasonry aimed to strike a balance between the promotion of good governance and the right to resist unjust political rulers, as proposed by the political philosopher Locke, among others. If an individual freemason took up this latter right, it would not bring an end to his masonic membership. Taken together with subtle references elsewhere in

The Constitutions, freemasonry makes a clear statement against philosophers such as Hobbes or Filmer, who argued for absolute and coercive state power derived from an indisputable divine authority. Instead, *The Constitutions* argues that freemasonry (possibly as representative of any community governed by a political system) will develop best within a system providing a balance between freedom of action and compliance with a given political power.

The third charge positions the lodge as being at the centre of any masonic activity. The lodge is the basic unit 'where masons assemble and work'. Rules of membership are also outlined. The fourth charge highlights meritocracy as the prime factor for promotion within freemasonry; however, 'it is impossible to describe these things [the nature of "merit"] in writing'. Rules for masonic work and conduct, clearly influenced by craft ordinances, are outlined in the fifth charge. Finally, the sixth charge with its six sub-divisions contains detailed rules of behaviour for inside and outside the lodge (in public), towards strangers, within the family and neighbourhood, and towards unknown freemasons.

The second behavioural rule is of some interest, since it exemplifies the practical implications of the first two charges on religion and politics. Quarrels about religion, nationality, or state politics are not to be brought into the lodge room since freemasons are of the 'catholick religion above-mention'd' (note that 'catholic' is used here to mean 'all-embracing'); and 'we are also of all nations, tongues, kindreds and languages, and are resolv'd against all Politicks', since the latter has never been for the good of the lodge 'nor ever will'. It is said that this rule gained particular significance after the Reformation and secession from Rome. In practical terms, modern freemasonry thus opened itself up to members from different Christian creeds, as long as they subscribed to the religious ideas of the first charge and abstained from discussing religion in the lodge. Despite (or because of) this tolerance for different varieties of Christian beliefs, the Catholic

Church condemned freemasonry as a heresy from 1738 onward. The exact extent of the 'Politicks' prohibited in the second behavioural rule is not entirely clear, but the discussion of daily political events and issues was certainly prohibited. This rule is cosmopolitan in its outlook, since freemasonry unites members from all nations and cultures. This anti-political stance may also have been influenced by Epicurean philosophy: to stay outside the corrupting logics of public politics and, rather, privately 'live in the concealed' ('lathe biosas').

Secrecy and society

As it entered the 18th century and drawing upon its earlier intellectual legacy, freemasonry very pointedly engaged with the nascent scientific culture of the early Enlightenment in general and with Newtonian science in particular. Throughout Europe, freemasons actively promoted scientific culture and counted scientists among their members. *The Constitutions* mention 'arts' and 'science' as synonyms for freemasonry. Ramsay's 'Discours' suggested an edition of a universal dictionary of sciences and arts. A tract written in defence of masonry claimed that masonic lodges are 'eminently styled as academies'. With this clear support, freemasonry placed itself at the core of a new culture of knowledge, replacing prejudice and speculation with evidence and experimentation. Scholars such as Margaret C. Jacob argue that freemasonry not only formulated liberal concepts for its organization, but also acted as a proto-democratic and egalitarian 'school of government' in which men (and some women) could learn skills fundamental to new forms of society, beyond the feudal logic and hierarchy that still governed most European states at the time.

This commitment is, however, difficult to align with the proclivity for mythology, secrecy, and ritual that is so prevalent in freemasonry. To sort out this potential tension, it is necessary to engage with the secrets and secrecy as representing a core distinguishing and organizing principle and as a structuring element for the transmission of masonic knowledge. The programmatic songs in *The Constitutions* speak of 'secrets of the art' and that 'the world is in pain our secrets to gain'; one of the verses reads:

> Whose Art transcends the common View?
> Their Secrets, ne'er to Strangers yet expos'd,
> Preserv'd shall be By Masons Free,
> And only to the ancient Lodge disclos'd;
> Because they're kept in Masons Heart
> By Brethren of the Royal Art.

Another verse claims that just as men are distinguished from animals, freemasons exceed their fellow humans because 'what's in knowledge choice and rare' is kept securely within a freemason's breast.

These few lines already establish the basic sociological function of secrecy that, furthermore, has a constitutive dimension in the internal transmission of knowledge. For members, who are in possession of (real or imagined) secrets that are only to be transmitted inside the lodge, a line is drawn between freemasons and non-freemasons; between 'us' and 'them'. These secrets, which are never to be revealed to strangers (or significant others), are in effect privileged knowledge, and represent art that 'transcends the common view', distinguishing freemasons from their fellow human beings. The avoidance of unplanned transmission of such privileged knowledge places a huge responsibility upon the individual freemason in the form of secrecy and silence.

Swiss sociologist Georg Simmel identified the ability for secrecy as 'one of the greatest accomplishments of humanity'. Simmel claims that human relationships are determined by the amount of knowledge we share with each other. Whether done willingly or unwillingly, a withholding of information from others is a necessary part of modern reality. Acceptance of how much we do not (need to) know about another individual determines the level of interpersonal trust in modern society. In this intricate play between opacity and transparency, information that some have that is seen to be withheld from the many appears to possess a special value. Furthermore, according to Simmel, every superior aspect of personality or performance that is seen to exceed that of the average person is felt to represent something mysterious.

Both these propositions lead people to believe 'that every secret is something essential and significant'. As such, there is a tension created to reveal what is secret. To keep a secret from others requires psychological fortitude—so great is the human need to communicate and thereby release the tension of concealment. Simmel believes that the amount of secrecy in all societies is more or less constant but expressed in different ways. As such, the more transparent a state becomes in public matters, the more secrecy (or privacy) is allowed to its citizens; leeway of action is created in private space.

As discussed earlier, freemasonry claims to possess privileged secrets and to transmit them internally. According to the narrative of *The Constitutions*, knowledge (transcending that of the average person) has been handed down via an uninterrupted chain of initiates from biblical times. These initiates have each then had to endure pressure both externally from others in their society and internally from their own human need to communicate with others and share these secrets. However, a good freemason keeps his privileged knowledge to himself; a central element of the masonic oaths is about keeping secrets from the uninitiated, from the 'profane', and from women in particular.

What, then, are the functions of secrecy in modern freemasonry? One is to bind the (until recent times, male) members to the secrets which must only be communicated through the performance of ritual or other normative masonic instruction.

Images, narratives, and myths in this regard are used to establish a sense of transcendence, of providing a superior observation point, and with it a sense of exclusivity. It relies on the idea that freemasonry is about a select chain of initiates—and that these sage (usually) men, who are highly versed in the sciences and arts (particularly geometry and architecture) of their time, will then transfer uncorrupted knowledge that will flow down through the different eras of human history.

German Egyptologist Jan Assmann studied the reinvention of Egyptian religion among the elites of the Enlightenment. He described the phenomenon of this new interest in pagan tradition 'religio duplex', whereby one secret religion was shared by the privileged (in this case, the elites were also in the masonic brotherhood) while a diversity of other religions were still being shared by the ordinary man. Freemasons saw themselves as representing a group that was a global, united, egalitarian, initiated, and exclusive male elite, which had set itself the task of building a better society for humankind. This taint of self-conscious elitism, even hubris, has haunted freemasonry ever since.

A second, more abstract and (possibly initially) unintended, function of secrecy is to prepare masonic initiates for life in modern society which has created a hitherto unprecedented level of anonymity and privacy. As Simmel argued, differentiation (initially in the Enlightenment period, of religion) in society has led to a loss of close and transparent interpersonal relations. Teaching secrecy to individuals is a way of accustoming them to a socio-economic reality of greater opacity/privacy, thus enabling them to navigate a society in which the creation of mutual trust is via increasingly abstract and detached means.

Last but not least, it is possible to read an indirect political dimension into the masonic insistence on secrecy. *The Constitutions* stress freedom of action for freemasonry in relation to political rule. Following Simmel's argument, in authoritarian and opaque states, citizens are allowed less privacy and secrecy; when state power augments the amount of transparency in their governance, individual privacy and right to secrecy increases. By actively claiming a right to individual privacy and secrecy, freemasonry challenges all forms of non-transparent and coercive government, and particularly those that shroud their power in mystery (and secrecy). It is therefore no wonder that freemasonry has clashed with authoritarian forms of government throughout the centuries—whether absolutist, papal, or other religiously and ideologically charged political systems.

Freemasonry reflected a need felt in society to hold onto the right to secrecy during charged political times. However, by the end of the 18th century, it was already being argued that in the age of Enlightenment it was unnecessary to retain this level of secrecy; that humanity had made such progress, that knowledge could now be shared with everyone. During the subsequent century, masonic reform movements did indeed alter the formulation and gravity of the masonic oath to secrecy, in some instances even abolishing it completely. Today, in response to a persistent accusation of conspiracy, masonic organizations have adopted a hitherto unprecedented policy of extensive transparency.

Philanthropy, charity, and cosmopolitanism

Although *The Constitutions* clearly place freemasonry within a distinctly British tradition, its general character is described as universal and inclusive, particularly in the 'Charges'. Not only is freemasonry linked to all major intellectual traditions of antiquity, but it claims that the 'religion in which all men agree' can be embraced by everyone, regardless of nationality or confession. Freemasonry promotes peace and opposes war. In Ramsay's 'Discours', this position is taken even further: he states that political rulers are incapable of establishing lasting institutions for the benefit of humankind as a whole. Not even the revered legislators of antiquity were able to create durable establishments, no matter how intelligent their laws may have been. They were incapable of expanding over all countries and making a lasting impact throughout the ages. Taken in perspective, Ramsay says, their laws were little more than military violence and the dominance of one people over another, and—since they were not based on general philanthropy—were never universal and did not conform to the taste, genius, or interest of all nations. Badly understood love of one's own country destroys one's love for humanity in general. Based on history, political rulers with a view for the particular interests of their nation have not been able to exercise good governance.

A failed state engages in military aggression, the violent expansion of its territory, hegemony, and exaggerated patriotism. Each nation has its own qualities, however:

> men are not to be essentially distinguished by the difference of tongues which they speak, of clothes which they wear, of countries which they inhabit, nor of dignities with which they are ornamented: the whole world is no other than one great republic, of which each nation is a family, and each individual a child.

In this view, there are only three levels of political relation, in principle: the individual, as a member of its national family; the family, as a branch of the world republic; and the world republic itself. Ramsay goes on to state that it was to revive and reanimate these maxims (borrowed from nature as representing a normative authority) that freemasonry was established. Equipped with this cosmopolitan ethos, the interest of the fraternity could be expanded to the entire human race; all nations could then increase their knowledge, creating a world without jealousy and discord, with individuals neither forgetting nor remembering too intensely the place where they were born. Ramsay's links between the chivalric orders and freemasonry were not only intended to induce a medieval legacy. He claims that the crusaders aimed to unite in one fraternity the subjects of all nations and thus create a 'spiritual nation' where a new people would be created, 'cemented by virtue and science'. For Ramsay, the ultimate manifestation of such a union is the publication of a universal dictionary of all liberal arts and useful sciences, so that 'the lights of all nations will be united in a single work'.

Ramsay's ideas on world citizenship can be interpreted as follows: in his view, the concord between human beings is rooted in the natural state of humanity. When political leadership interfered in this state of nature by means of aggressive and coercive expansion, the true unanimity of humans was lost. By embracing a morality that can be experienced by everybody, today's freemasons aim at a revival of the true state of nature, and work with the same ambitions as their ancestors to create a new people engaging with universal solidarity in an imagined community of a world republic. The roots of this universal solidarity are not only found in a common spiritual/mythical past, but also in the intellectual challenges of the future: to collect, augment, and disseminate knowledge for the benefit of humankind as a whole.

It may be important to note that this part of Ramsay's 'Discours' was printed in masonic periodicals, first in the USA in 1788 and then in London in 1795 (and again in 1797–8), under the headings 'The influence of free masonry upon society' and 'Social influence of Freemasonry'. In the 1780s, a masonic journal in Vienna had already made calls for the adoption of cosmopolitan values as representing a moral duty for every freemason. Ramsay stated that the legislators of the past had failed in their efforts since they had been unable to expand philanthropy to all of humankind. This perspective of freemasonry has carried implications for the position of charity as one of the major elements of masonic thought (and of the ethics of action) ever since. In freemasonry, charity is seen as an almost foundational *raison d'être* and has been invoked as a proof of the movement's innocence when faced with the suspicions of outsiders. Since its inception, freemasonry has been involved in fundraising for charitable purposes in education, medical care, and culture.

One element of masonic charity is internal solidarity; drawing on medieval guild ordinances, modern freemasonry preserved the principle of self-help in times of illness and distress. This principle has contributed to the persistent perceptions of outsiders that freemasons favour each other in their activities outside of the lodge as well as within it. External masonic charity largely falls into two categories: reactive and proactive. Reactive charity simply aims to relieve a pressing need in the short term (as a Christian duty), whereas proactive charity anticipates and seeks to avoid future misfortune in the long term (an enlightened concept of self-mastery as represented by French thinker and possible freemason Condorcet, for example).

A majority of masonic charity initiatives in the 18th century were of the latter character. Freemasons raised funds to establish orphanages, schools, and hospitals, and promoted the use of inoculation against smallpox. For all its chivalric imagination during the 18th century, the Strict Observance attempted to create a pan-European pension fund for its members and engaged in a number of economic ventures to create financial security (including colonial and industrial projects). The stranded economic plans of the Strict Observance were among the main reasons for its failure. At the turn of the 19th century, many philanthropic freemasons engaged in the establishment of banks and insurance companies, and in reforming school education. With growing industrialization and the emergence of mass society, masonic charity assumed another character. Some grand lodges called for the direct involvement of freemasonry in social issues, while others retained the more private philanthropic approach of the previous century. These different views on societal commitment created and perpetuated a dividing line between different forms of freemasonry that has lasted to the current day.

Chapter 5
From darkness to light

Live performance of ritual constitutes the centrepiece of activities in freemasonry and is one of the defining features that distinguish it from the majority of other associations. The rituals of freemasonry developed during the 18th and 19th centuries and have since remained unchanged in their general design. Masonic rituals take place inside (and partly outside) the lodge according to a more or less predefined script (the ritual text) as a dramatizing performance in ritual and real time—much like a musical score and a concert, or a play and its performance. Rituals fulfil three major functions: initiation (establishing a demarcation between the internal and external worlds), the transmission of further knowledge at higher or deeper levels in the insider's community of knowledge (performing the emblematic function), and investiture in a particular office or status. The initiate or candidate and his experience is at the centre of ritual performance. In a Western context, ceremonies in freemasonry are one of the rare secular instances that involve the practice of rituals of initiation.

Ritual is an integral feature of human cultures across the globe. The most common understanding of ritual in cultural studies is that rituals are celebrated at the passing through or transition between significant stages in individual or collective life biographies, such as adolescence, marriage, and death. These rituals follow a common structure: in the first phase, the previous life stage or position is left behind (separation); in the second phase, a state of transition between the old and new states is established (liminal); and in the third and final phase, the integration into a new state (incorporation) as a form of re-birth is accomplished. In the liminal phase, the rules of 'normality' do not apply; the candidate—often in an altered state of consciousness—frequently encounters a surreal world that is turned upside down and in which his character is supposed to change.

However, a strong non-Western bias has existed in cultural studies, in that rituals of initiation (Figure 5) have long been associated with 'traditional' cultures. It is only comparatively recently that scholars have directed their attention towards Western esotericism and thus freemasonry and other initiatory societies. In short, Western esotericism circles around the individual effort to gain spiritual knowledge, confronting the individual with divine aspects of existence.

As derived from medieval guild practices, freemasons originally only practised rather straightforward rituals related to admission, fellowship (which often included travelling for a specific period of time), and mastery, with huge variation in rituals between different countries. By 1725, however, an elaborate three-degree system of Entered Apprentice, Fellow Craft, and Master Mason was in place in England. From around 1730, and certainly from 1740 onwards, additional higher degrees were added. Historically, particular sets of degree structures have been organized into specific 'rites', which serve as defining features that distinguish between different masonic bodies.

Masonic rituals are placed within a symbolic narrative framework pointing progressively forward through the degree structure. In the lodge room, the ritual is framed by opening and closing rites, marking the start and end of the ritual ceremony. The purpose

5. **Initiation: the apprentice receives the light** (end of 19th century).

of these rites is to establish a secret and sacred space that is delimited from the outside world, and a symbolic time (different from real time) in which the ritual unfolds. The interior of the lodge must be arranged with special furniture and symbolic items; thus, a three-dimensional virtual space—an 'other world'—is created for the performance of ritual. The ritual, in turn, is impossible without the interaction of several freemasons dressed in special regalia, along with the most important among them, the officers of the lodge. Their lines and words in the ritual (which frequently take the format of an exchange of questions and answers), and when and how these are spoken, bring the ritual play to life (transforming space and time), along with symbolic gestures and movements performed inside the lodge. Apart from the officers of the lodge, who hold a direct ritual function, the attending freemasons are integrated into the ritual play but generally remain third-party spectators.

Rituals are primarily enacted for the individual initiate or candidate (or sometimes a group of them) and his (or their) experience (see Figure 5). Self-initiation is impossible. The ritual has a preparatory phase outside the lodge, followed by a ritual entrance into the lodge, with further events then occurring inside. The candidate receives tokens related to his new status and is instructed about the symbolism of the degree or (as in the case with *The Constitutions*) on some moral or mythological aspect of freemasonry. As a rule, lodge meetings are followed by a meal, which is also more or less ritualized. Rituals for the transfer of new knowledge at a deeper level or of investiture follow the same general pattern.

Within this basic performative structure (see Box 1), the variety of content for different degrees is in theory unlimited. As such, masonic rituals resemble other typical form-bound expressions of baroque culture, such as the classical symphony with its relatively fixed arrangement of consecutive movements. Since the 18th century, a plethora of fraternal orders have copied the ritual pattern of freemasonry and filled it with arbitrary—even ironic or mocking—content.

Another way of understanding masonic ritual is to consider the rhetoric and emblematic tradition of freemasonry, which, as has been discussed, is derived from the Renaissance revival of antiquity. Depending on which authors or schools of rhetoric it comes from, the development and performance of a piece of oration is divided into different parts, such as: invention, the disposition, and the division of arguments (i.e. the opening, in which a statement of the case is made; the proof of the case through examples; recapitulation; and a final statement), and style and delivery.

The candidate and what he is exposed to can thus be likened to the argumentation of an orator: the candidate (i.e. the subject

Box 1 Structure of masonic rituals of initiation

1. Opening of the lodge (without the initiate present).
2. Preparation of candidates for initiation (outside the lodge).
3. Entry into the lodge (after candidates have responded to questions).
4. Circumambulations around the lodge (during which the candidates are put to the test).
5. Taking an oath of secrecy and fidelity (with penalties spelled out).
6. Formal admission to the degree (acceptance into the community).
7. Instruction in the secrets/teaching of the degree (questions and answers, oration).
8. Receiving visible tokens, a symbolical name or motto of the degree (marking internal hierarchy).
9. Closing of the lodge (with initiates present).
10. 'Table lodge' (formal dinner).

Comment: Although a table lodge almost always is a feature of masonic lodge meetings, it is disputable whether it is a part of the ritual or not; however, on the level of formal sociability, it certainly is.

(Adapted from Henrik Bogdan, *Western Esotericism and Rituals of Initiation* 2007, Table 2.1.)

of the oration, which is expounded in a pre-planned schedule of arguments) serves as a living example of the statement that is being made. If this idea of the ritual as a piece of rhetoric is united with the emblematic component of the ritual, the lodge room then functions as a physical backdrop within which emblematic situations are three-dimensionally staged. That said, it is obvious that the bodily experience of ritual is of paramount importance in the process. In performance theory, this has been called an 'engrammatic effect'. Theatre scholar Kristiane Hasselmann argues that the repeated physical experience of the masonic ritual drama is inscribed into the body and accustoms the candidate to certain behaviour in society—a so-called 'habitus'.

The craft degrees of freemasonry

In 1730, the first full exposure of all three craft degrees in freemasonry was published: *Masonry Dissected*. The thirty-odd paged brochure eventually appeared in more than thirty editions and was disseminated in translations and in periodicals across Europe. Despite the negative view of modern freemasonry given in the preface by its author Samuel Prichard, research suggests that *Masonry Dissected* was used as an aide memoire by existing lodges. Our knowledge about the degrees practised in masonic rituals before 1730 is light. Just like *Masonry Dissected*, the texts are catechisms, preserved as manuscripts or even items printed in the periodical press. Masonic catechisms are presented as questions and answers between the master of the lodge (or any other designated officer) and an initiated member. These questions test the member's knowledge of the symbolism and basic concepts of freemasonry, the practical course of initiation (or other rituals performed), and the content of the masonic oath. Therefore, it is only indirectly possible to reconstruct the script according to which masonic ritual unfolded in terms of when and where. From 1737 onward, exposures of masonic rituals are more descriptive in nature. The first full publication that included 'stage directions' was a work entitled *L'Ordre des Franc-Maçons trahi et le secret des Mopses revelée*, which appeared in 1745 in Amsterdam and was immediately translated into other European languages. During the same year, the first comprehensive visual exposure also appeared: a series of seven engravings providing detailed insights into the staging of the ritual.

According to *Masonry Dissected*, the Entered Apprentice degree introduces members to symbols of masonry and their interpretation, to a true understanding of the ritual, and to the oath that is taken. A specific part of the degree outlines the design and meaning of the lodge as a symbolic place in space and time. It is apparent that the lodge is taught as being originally located in Jerusalem ('in the Vale of Josaphat'). Initiation into the first degree is thus mainly about entering a new community of knowledge, and achieving familiarity with a specific set of symbols and the symbolic settings of the lodge itself.

The degree of Fellow Craft states that the candidate is familiar with the letter 'G', standing for geometry as the 'fifth science' (in the medieval canon of liberal arts). The candidate is now a builder in the Temple of Solomon, and the catechism makes explicit references to 1 Kings 7:1–51. As a fellow, the candidate is admitted to the middle chamber of the temple (suggesting a hierarchy of location); here, a second and divine meaning of the letter 'G' is revealed, referring to 'the Grand Architect or Contriver of the Universe'. This letter and its symbolic meaning are spelled out. Compared to expectations for the Entered Apprentice degree, the fellow is now expected to handle more advanced knowledge, as the science of geometry leads him closer to divinity.

In the first degree, the candidate is asked 'From whence come you?', whereupon he replies 'From the Holy Lodge of St John's'. This explicitly Christian reference is explained in a commentary to the second degree that deserves to be quoted here in full:

> The reason why they denominate themselves of the Holy Lodge of St. John's, is, because he was the Fore-runner of our Saviour, and laid the first Parallel Line to the Gospel.

Whatever is specifically intended by this formulation, it clearly states that the Old Testament setting of the two first degrees points forward to the New Testament. Moreover, Prichard goes on to state (and ridicule) that some do assert that 'our Saviour himself was accepted as a Free-Mason whilst he was in the Flesh'.

The Master's degree introduces a completely new motif: the master's task is 'to seek for that which was lost and is now found', which is 'the Master-Mason's Word'. This word, the catechism goes on, was lost with the death of the Temple architect (in French ritual families, the Temple architect is called Adoniram). Now follows the first version of the so-called 'Hiramic legend', which has been called the most important myth in freemasonry and which is not only the pinnacle of the first three degrees, but the starting point of a number of subsequent higher degrees. The Hiramic legend is an apocryphal continuation of the account of the construction of Solomon's Temple in the Bible.

In Prichard's version, Hiram inspects the Temple in the middle of the day. Three Fellow Craft masons place themselves at the three entrances to the Temple in order to demand the Master's Word from the architect. When he denies them the Word, each of them strikes Hiram with a tool until he finally dies. The murderers temporarily hide the body in the Temple. In the middle of the night, they carry Hiram out of the Temple and bury him on a hill. Fifteen days later, fifteen freemasons sent out by Solomon on a search mission find the decayed body of the architect. Since they fail to find the Master's Word with or on him, they agree to adopt the first word spoken at the discovery of the corpse, which is eventually given as 'Macbenah'. The discovery of the body is announced to Solomon, who orders Hiram's body to be carried back to the Temple. When exhuming the corpse, Hiram is raised by the 'five points of fellowship': hand to hand, foot to foot, cheek to cheek, knee to knee, and hand in back. Finally, Hiram is buried in the Sanctum Sanctorum of the Temple.

Ritual scholar Jan Snoek has identified no fewer than fifty varieties of the Hiramic legend; a more influential version than Prichard's was the version published in *L'Ordre des Franc-Maçons trahi*. Prichard's exposure provides no clue as to whether or how the Hiramic legend was staged as a ritual. However, *L'Ordre* (and its visualization) describes the ceremony extensively. On a rectangular carpet (called a 'tracing board' in freemasonry) placed on the floor of the lodge room, are the following images: a coffin surrounded by tears and framed by the image of a skull and crossed bones. In front of the coffin lies an opened ruler, and behind the coffin is a square; to the right, a hill with a twig of acacia is displayed. The tracing board is marked on each side with the four symbolic points of the compass and lit by nine candles: three in the east, three in the south, and three in the west. The initiate is brought brusquely into the lodge room and, after a short walk, placed in front of the tracing board. He is made to walk over the symbolic coffin with three big steps, during which he is hit with a soft item to imitate the strikes Hiram received. With his gavel, the master of the lodge symbolically knocks the candidate's forehead, after which the candidate is laid down upon the shape of the coffin. A bloodstained shroud is placed over the face of the candidate. The attending freemasons form a circle around the candidate and point towards him with their swords. The master of the lodge raises the candidate as Hiram is described to have been raised, and words of fright are exclaimed. The bloodstained shroud is removed and the ritual finished.

The initiate thus takes the position of Hiram and is ritualistically killed in the same manner. Covered in the shroud, a provisional grave, he awaits discovery by his fellow masters. The corpse is found and eventually raised, which is why freemasonry refers to the third-degree ceremony as being 'raised as a Master'. Obviously, the ritual identifies the candidate with the Temple architect, as the unselfish hero of the narrative who is willing to sacrifice himself, but there is yet another dimension. The hero turns out to be a deity, and the candidate is mysteriously united with him (through 'unio mystica', which also refers to a tradition of strong emotional identification with Christ).

In what sense does Hiram represent a deity? Firstly, he is obviously in possession of the blueprint of the Temple (which is the design of God, according to 1 Chronicles 28:19) and of the knowledge of how to pronounce the Master's Word. Secondly, he is buried in the Sanctum Sanctorum, the 'Holy of Holies'. In Jewish tradition, the Sanctum Sanctorum is the innermost part of the Temple where the presence of God reveals itself and where nobody but the High Priest is allowed to enter—and only on one day of the year, Yom Kippur (the Day of Atonement). It was during this ceremony that the Tetragrammaton (YHWH) was pronounced. However, according to one interpretation, the proper way of spelling out the name of God by inserting vowels into the Tetragrammaton fell into oblivion during the Babylonian Captivity, which of course can be likened to the loss of (the skill to pronounce) the Master's Word after the killing of Hiram. 'To seek for that which was lost and is now found' thus potentially assumes a religious meaning. Another reading is that the correct pronunciation of the Tetragrammaton has been retained, but that it cannot be used since there is no Temple left where it can be spelled out.

If, according to the entirely apocryphal masonic legend, Hiram is buried in the old Temple that was eventually destroyed, it furthermore brings up the question of if and when he could potentially be rediscovered at an unspecified point in the future. For any freemason who was familiar with the Christian tradition, Christ was seen as the new temple that eventually will be erected for humankind. Reading the Hiramic legend together with the explanation given in Prichard about St John, who lays the first parallel line to the Gospel, leaves little doubt that Hiram and Christ are intended to be identical from the outset. However, with growing secularization, this obviously Christian link to the third-degree ritual was toned down. As with most elements in masonic ritual, the personification of the Temple architect is open to multiple readings, and an explicitly Judeo-Christian interpretation is not an absolute necessity.

In evolved versions of the ritual, the candidate is initially suspected of being one of the Fellow Craft masons who killed

Hiram, opening up an intriguing double identification. Thus, the candidate is first associated with the perpetrator of meaningless violence and then with its victim. In the French versions of the ritual, Hiram is buried with the Tetragrammaton engraved upon a gold (or silver) triangle on his tomb, which reinforces his identification with God. Religious historian Henrik Bogdan suggests that the search for the lost vowels of the Tetragrammaton can clearly be related to Jewish cabalistic traditions (the Zohar), which also aim at an individual experience of the Godhead via a 'unio mystica'. For Renaissance practitioners of Kabbalah, this implied a search for and identification with Christ. YHWH conceals the name of Jesus, which can be found by the insertion of the Hebrew letter 'Shin'. Seen from this perspective, the third-degree ritual in freemasonry has apparent traces of cabalistic influence.

In the middle of the 19th century, a considerably darker and more esoteric version of the Hiramic legend was disseminated in theosophical circles. In his *Le Voyage en orient* (1851) the French proto-surrealist writer Gérard de Nerval recounts the Temple legend by introducing the Queen of Sheba or Balkis (known in all Abrahamic religions), who visited Solomon in Jerusalem, according to the Bible. Following *Le Voyage en orient*, Sheba falls in love with Solomon for his wisdom, particularly because of their elaborate exchange of riddles (which, with their extremely allegorical language, strongly resemble masonic catechisms). But then she meets Hiram, the Temple architect, and adores his skills as a craftsman and his position as leader of an immense workforce. She turns her love towards Hiram, while Solomon is gripped by morbid jealousy and plots to kill the architect. Before this is effected, Hiram and Balkis confess their love to each other and, in an evolved version of the legend, Hiram entrusts the secret Master's Word to her (this might also refer to her pregnancy). In one scene of the legend, Hiram descends to the underworld, where he learns in the sanctuary of fire that he is related to Tubal-Cain, the father of ingenuity and industriousness.

The freedom-loving Cainites (represented by Hiram) are thus positioned against the descendants of Abel (represented by Solomon), who impose a tyranny of cold and calculating imagination and ideas upon humankind.

Nerval's version of the Hiramic legend was picked up by the anthroposophist Rudolf Steiner, who assigns to it a pivotal significance in his lecture cycle, 'The Temple legend' (1904–6). Other traditions claim that Balkis actually gave birth to a child of Solomon, named Menelik. This royal descent was a constitutive part of the Ethiopian national mythology up to Haile Selassie, and has in turn influenced Rastafarian religion. Given the prominence of the encounter between Balkis and Solomon in Renaissance art and literature, its virtual absence in masonic traditions (apart from some references in 'Antients' sources) begs further explanation.

Development and motives of higher degrees

The narrative of the Hiramic legend obviously has the potential for further progressive elaboration. The degrees described in the following section are historically the first continuations from which all other higher degree systems evolved. Some varieties of third-degree rituals already included the search for and punishment of the perpetrators. This part of the extended legend was isolated and turned into a separate degree ('Maître Elu' or Elect Master). Solomon elects a number of Master Masons to the task of searching for Hiram, sending them out to find his murderers and avenge the crime committed. Eventually, the content of this vengeance degree, also called *Kadosh*, was merged with a chivalric and—more specifically—a Templar motif (the Sublime Order of Elect Knights). This degree reveals that the elected masters are in fact the surviving members of the Knights Templar, who had been disbanded as a result of an injustice. In parallel to the vengeance of Hiram, the sublime knights now promise to avenge the death of their innocent grand master, Jacques de Molay, burned at the stake in Paris in March 1314.

However, the Hiramic legend also continued in a different manner. The Temple of Solomon was eventually destroyed. After seventy years of captivity in Babylon, King Cyrus allowed the Israelites to return and to re-build the Temple under the leadership of Zerubbabel. This Biblical episode forms the backdrop to another (fourth) degree of freemasonry, the 'Royal Arch' or 'Scottish Master', which overlap in apocryphal and mythical content. In the ritual legend, the Royal Arch initiate is identified with three so-called 'sojourners' of noble (possibly Kohen) origin, who offer Zerubbabel assistance in re-building the temple. While clearing the temple grounds, they discover pillars and eventually an archway under which a secret vault is located.

Lifting two keystones, one of the sojourners is lowered into the vault with a rope and discovers a scroll. When more sunlight allows it, he also finds a pedestal in the form of an altar 'with certain mystic characters engraven thereupon' and a veil covering the upper part of the altar. The sojourner lifts the veil and assumes that he now has discovered the 'Sacred and Mysterious Name itself' (which, according to one reading, was lost with the Babylonian Captivity). The ritual confirms that it is indeed the name of God, to be pronounced by the High Priest on Yom Kippur, and that the candidate is thus initiated into sacerdotal knowledge. Although firmly based on the imaginative world of the Old Testament, there are hints forecasting a Christian reading. In the lodge room of the Royal Arch, the insignia of the twelve tribes of Israel are displayed; among these are four principal banners with four winged creatures: man, lion, ox, and eagle, symbols that were associated with the Four Evangelists. It is also explained that the symbols of the pickaxe, crow, and shovel used during the ritual point to the final judgement.

The earliest known so-called 'Scottish Master' degrees tell a slightly different story. The candidate is informed that Hiram was in fact a priest. During the ritual, the candidate is purified like a

Levite and finally—like a (Kohen) High Priest—admitted to the Sanctum Sanctorum. Asked by the master of the lodge, 'Are you a Scottish Master?', the candidate replies 'No one prevents me from walking into the Sanctum Sanctorum whenever I wish to'. The setting of the ritual is the destroyed temple, symbolized by two broken columns that form a St Andrew's cross, beneath which is placed a symbol with four circles and squares. In the next part of the intricate ritual, the candidate is dubbed a knight of St Andrew, the patron saint of Scotland. The mythological legend of the degree is told in a similar fashion to that of the Royal Arch, but with a completely different setting. The search for the lost Master's Word also forms the centrepiece of the ritual; however, it takes place during the time of the Crusades.

In Jerusalem, the freemasons unite themselves with the Order of St John and together clear up the site of the Old Temple. As in the Royal Arch legend, in the midst of the rubble they find the original location of the Sanctum Sanctorum, with four square and four circular stones, four cups of pure gold, and four pillars of ore. Under the last of the stones, the lost Master's Word is inscribed. These stones, the legendary account goes on to say, were transported to Scotland after the Crusades. In evolved versions of the Scottish Master's degree, the chivalric Masons find a vault and from there exhume the coffin of Hiram, which contains a number of items such as the original blueprint of the Temple.

A further development of the Hiramic legend unfolds in so-called Mark Masonry, which was practised for the first time around 1770. In fact, the Mark degree is strictly seen only as a continuation of the Fellow degree, ritualizing the account of 1 Kings (and *The Constitutions*) and appointing Fellow Masons as overseers of the work, or 'Harodim'. A Mark Mason also chooses his individual masonic mark (referring back to the praxis of medieval masons, which was to carve a symbolic sign into the stones they worked with).

Taken together, the ritual continuations of the Hiramic legend build a bridge from its Old Testament origins straight into the Middle Ages and the Knights Templar mythology in freemasonry. Whereas the Elect Master and Royal Arch can be understood as a religious sequel within the framework of sacred mythology, the Scottish Master and Elect Knights create a link to the secular history of pretended or real orders of medieval knighthood. The underlying narrative pattern is that of progression combined with the promise of potential transformation, ennoblement, and redemption. Higher degrees thus offer refined knowledge in a principally spiritual quest as well as an artificial or substitute mythology and religion (compared to mainstream Catholic or Protestant religion), paired with latent societal activism. With chivalric and sacerdotal elements thus in place, the foundation was laid for the future development of an innumerable variety of higher degrees. A masonic encyclopaedia published in 1961 lists the names of more than a thousand degrees, although most of these are no longer practised.

Masonic rites between inclusion, delimitation, and authority

The sequence of rituals establishes a progressive programme of moral self-improvement. These programmes of prescribed actions or practices of ceremony were eventually standardized under the authority of specific masonic bodies, grand lodges, or orders representing sets of particular 'rites' or 'systems'. Throughout the history of freemasonry, the authority over this programme of rituals was (and to some extent still is) a disputed issue. The major fault line was established between the first three and all subsequent degrees. Craft masonry claimed authority in form and content only over the first three degrees. When the two rival English grand lodges of 'Antients' and 'Moderns' were united in 1813, the Royal Arch degree (principally practised by the 'Antients') was officially declared a completion of the third degree, whereas in other rites it was clearly seen as a separate fourth degree.

In Britain and by extension in the British colonies and the USA, the authority over the first three degrees rests with territorial grand lodges, with the Royal Arch constituting a borderline case. Other degrees, such as those conferred in Mark Masonry, developed their own organizations. Today, there are around twenty of these so-called 'appendant bodies' in England and Wales. The situation in the Americas is similar.

The 18th-century proclivity towards opulence in form contributed to a rapid development of different ritual systems. Originally, freemasonry only worked with the first three degrees, but from 1740 onwards, the higher degrees were added as continuations or were practised by separate lodges or orders. During the 1750s, the first successful attempts were launched to organize progressive ritual programmes in coherent organizations. One prominent example is the so-called Strict Observance, which from 1751 onwards united the first three craft, the additional Scottish, and the supreme chivalric Templar degrees into one consecutive system on three separate levels. However, the system was not immune to change and allowed the integration of Templar priesthood degrees with rather esoteric content during the 1770s. After 1782, this threefold division of the degree structure was also introduced to the succeeding system of the Scottish Rectified Rite. Already in 1760, the threefold division was incorporated into the Swedish rite (with its eleven-degree system still existing today). In France, the higher degrees were also organized within the national GODF, thus creating a potential progression from the lowest to the highest degrees. Even the infamous Order of the Bavarian Illuminati was divided into three consecutive levels—however, the names and content of its supreme degrees varied considerably from those of the Templar systems.

The most prominent and widespread coherent system, in terms of membership and global distribution, is the AASR, which organizes thirty-three degrees on several levels. First established in 1801, its history and development in rituals stretches back to the 1760s.

Within freemasonry, there has been a profound division concerning the hierarchy, authority, meaning, and privilege of interpretation in relation to the higher degrees. The criticism of 'nuisance' of higher degrees culminated between 1780 and 1800, first in the collapse of the Templar system of the Strict Observance (1782) and finally in post-revolutionary conspiracy theories. These theories blamed the higher degrees for representing corrupt and degenerate forms of freemasonry with potentially revolutionary agendas. A strong masonic reform movement emerged and aimed to roll back the influence of higher degrees and their organizations, and to work in the 'pure' form of craft masonry only. At the same time, systems with integrated degree structures claimed to reveal the true meaning of the craft degrees at higher levels of knowledge. This conflict of hierarchy and interpretation foreshadowed the division between different forms of freemasonry during subsequent centuries, and particularly the division between 'humanitarian' and 'confessional' varieties.

Purpose of rituals

Given the pivotal position of rituals within freemasonry, it is legitimate to ask what purpose they fulfil. Firstly, rituals of initiation draw a line between the public and private sphere—between external and internal, secret and open. Hence, they are used to reinforce the idea of the secret and of secrecy as an organizational and knowledge principle in freemasonry. Secondly, it is in live performance, through the experience and application of ritual accompanied by strong sceneries, images, and metaphors, that masonic ideas are expressed and transferred to a candidate. It is only in cooperation between officers and lodge members that the ritual can actually take place. Masonic rituals and their dynamic expansion (within a pre-defined framework of constitutive elements) are a remarkable instance of invented autonomous programmes of moral and spiritual self-education centred on the individual and his quest. This quest takes place within the narrative structure of the construction of Solomon's Temple, the death of its architect, and the events unfolding thereafter. The Temple assumes the position of an image of the world ('imagus mundi') and is thus a metaphor for human society and its potential perfection. From the ruins, it can be reconstructed, in the form of a new Temple, as a cathedral, or in an entirely spiritual form.

No external ideological or political authorities imposed on freemasons (or any other fraternal orders) how to develop their rituals in form and content. These rituals are self-generated and original, initially framed around well-known Jewish-Christian mythologies and a classical legacy, but with a basic form of ritual play that was filled with the possibility of infinite variation. Physical experience (and artificially generated states of mind and consciousness) is an integrated part of the ritual drama, which inscribes itself onto the body. Repeated physical ritualistic staging aims at the internalization of moral behaviour patterns for application in everyday life. In the case of freemasonry, at least in the craft degrees, this internalization clearly relates to the central Enlightenment value of self-mastery in a society where there is ever increasing interpersonal complexity. However, the esoteric content of masonic rituals (such as the cabalistic influence in search of what is lost and the 'unio mystica') also places freemasonry in a position of resistance to the dominance of either doctrinal faith or pure rationality.

This side-stepping of doctrinal faith or pure rationality is exemplified by the third-degree ritual, which is a staged overcoming of mortality. By offering this experience to hundreds of thousands of members over the last three centuries, freemasonry has contributed to a shift in attitude over death. Many have turned from a previous concern with avoiding possible divine retribution in the afterlife towards a more secular doctrine—a concern rather with their future reputation in society after their demise.

Chapter 6
Organizational culture

The global success of freemasonry as a voluntary association lies in its well-organized internal structure. By 1723, the masonic foundational rules for organization had already been outlined and codified, and would last for centuries to come. Within a few decades, freemasonry had developed solid structures, from the local lodge to the regional/provincial level to the grand lodge at the national level, which in turn regulated relationships with grand lodges in other territories/countries.

From around 1720 onwards, the masonic movement spread quickly from London to the continent, representing a particularly British form of sociability at a time when Anglomania was in vogue. The English grand lodge, moreover, claimed the right to define and certify the 'regularity' of masonic bodies throughout Europe and the world, an ambition that intensified considerably after 1760. Within this concept of regularity, both ethical and organizational standards were defined, to which most of the masonic bodies in Europe voluntarily subscribed, although diverged from them at their own discretion. And it is important to stress this divergence, as freemasonry was never an international organization with a single headquarters, an overruling governing body, and a truly consistent ideology. As such freemasonry was adapted to a large variety of local contexts—religious as much as cultural—in the process of cultural transfer, with key features being seen across the globe.

As discussed earlier, the smallest organizational unit, the lodge, was ruled by a master and officers (who were elected in most cases) and it staged meetings in which new members were admitted by a ritual of initiation. Knowledge of freemasonry was conferred through a number of degrees (originally three, but considerably more later on) and through instructions and orations. A lodge would charge a membership fee and raise money by various other means for the carrying out of charitable projects. These projects were originally intended to assist members or relatives of the group who were in distress, but this was expanded over the centuries to include the wider society. Each lodge kept records of its meetings, correspondence, finances, and members, to whom certificates of membership were issued in order to facilitate mobility between the global network of lodges. Formal lodge meetings were generally followed by or contained a time of conviviality: a ritualized meal with rules for toasts and songs as well as formal openings and closings. Many lodges engaged in cultural events that would be open to the general public, such as concerts, theatre performances, balls, and other diversions. They also arranged public processions and ceremonies on the occasion of important festivities, the laying of foundation stones, and masonic funerals.

A lodge would normally seek formal approval ('constitution' through a warrant) from a higher masonic authority and then join that body as a corporate member, a (provincial) sub-branch. However, there are many examples of lodges and similar local units, both masonic and quasi-masonic, that have not followed this protocol of seeking approval. Regional formats of organization in lodges tend to be relatively transparent and consistent with each other, but on a more national or international level, the organizational principles become complex and at times contradictory, being affected by the political ambition and personal preferences of the lodge organizers.

Regularity and recognition

The thirty-nine paragraphs of General Regulations that were
appended to the 1723 version of *The Constitutions* included
detailed rules for individual lodges and for their grand lodge.
A lodge is also a decision-making body (here called a 'chapter')
that must keep a book with by-laws and a membership record.
A number of paragraphs outline membership requirements.
The regulations also detail the procedures for the establishment
of new lodges (a separate postscript describes the ceremonial
installation of a new lodge). Most of the paragraphs explain the
work of the grand lodge, which replicates the administrative
structure of individual lodges only on a larger (eventually
national) scale.

The grand lodge is a decision-making body to which individual
lodges send their representatives, who 'are supposed to speak their
mind' but be bound by a majority vote, which will feed into grand
lodge decision-making. New regulations can only be formed with
'the approbation and consent of the majority of all the brethren
present[, this] being absolutely necessary to make the same
binding and obligatory'. The election of a grand master and the
specified ceremonies surrounding these procedures are described
at length. A special paragraph explores the possibility of a grand
master abusing his power. The general tone of the regulations
underlines the freemasons' ambition to establish conformity in
praxis; for instance, paragraph XI states that 'all particular lodges
are to observe the same usages as much as possible' in order to
cultivate 'a good understanding among free-masons'.

From the outset, the 'premier' English grand lodge of 'Moderns'
reserved the right to establish new lodges and to act as the
regulatory body in its own territory. Soon after, grand lodges
were formed in Ireland and Scotland. Nonetheless, despite the
ambitions of these early grand lodges, competing masonic bodies

soon evolved in Britain. When the second edition of *The Constitutions* was published in 1738, Anderson mentioned the existence of grand lodges in the Netherlands, France, Germany, and Italy which had been formed following the English example but which had not necessarily been authorized by the English grand lodge. Some of these grand lodges were nonetheless regarded as English provinces. The French term 'Grand Orient' corresponds in organizational terms to a grand lodge. In masonic systems that have adopted a further hierarchy of chivalric degrees (such as in the Swedish rite), the national masonic bodies are as a rule called 'Orders'.

Matters grew in complexity when a rivalling grand lodge called 'the Antients' was formed in England in 1751. However, it wasn't until the 1760s that a more systematic attempt was made to control masonic international affairs and this was by the premier grand lodge of the 'Moderns'. This was occasioned by a second substantial boost in lodge establishments across Europe during the Seven Years War. It was at this time that the 'Moderns' started to formally recognize non-English grand lodges such as those of France, Sweden, and the Netherlands as independent organizations with their own respective national territory. It was also during the subsequent decades that the first serious international controversies relating to grand lodge authorization took place.

For example, the Swedish grand lodge, which had been established in 1760, cited a French charter from 1737, which was renewed in 1752, as providing the approval for their establishment. However, strictly speaking, the 'Moderns' had not yet authorized the French masonic bodies which had granted Sweden permission to form masonic lodges. This being the case, during the 1760s, a British diplomatic service secretary set up some masonic lodges in Sweden using a warrant he had received directly from London, and claimed that his lodges represented true masonic authority on Swedish territory. This created a split in Swedish freemasonry, finally resolved in 1771 to the advantage of the Swedish grand lodge. The correspondence relating to this dispute provides evidence of the masonic art in finding balance in issues under dispute.

An even more complex situation occurred with the German grand lodge, Grosse Landesloge der Freimaurer von Deutschland (GLL), which had originally received its constitution from Sweden in 1767—during the period when the authority and legitimacy of the Swedish grand lodge was being questioned. Sweden attempted to unite with the masonic rite of the Strict Observance (SO) during the late 1770s, but this competed with the GLL on German territory. Therefore, the negotiators of SO demanded Sweden withdraw its constitution of the GLL. The Swedish delegates complied with these demands; however, they were unaware that the GLL had in the meantime received a formal warrant from the 'Moderns' in England. Over the next few years, a massive diplomatic correspondence unfolded between the masonic houses of London, Berlin, and Stockholm—one that is yet to be edited and published.

These episodes demonstrate that international relations in freemasonry were a rather unregulated area with sometimes unexpected alliances. It was during the 19th century that the loose agreements between European (and American) grand lodges first developed into formal coalitions. The first serious split occurred during the 1870s, when the Belgian and French Grand Orients decided to abolish reference to a 'Grand Architect of the Universe' and to establish the principle of freedom of conscience in taking the masonic oath. The UGLE declared the GODF 'irregular' despite an absence of any clear-cut definition of regularity. However, it was only in 1929 that the 'home' grand lodges of England, Scotland, and Ireland agreed upon a document entitled the 'Basic Principles for Grand Lodge Recognition' that would define regularity. The document has eight points and was slightly amended in 1989 (see Box 2).

With these eight principles, the dividing line between 'regular' and 'irregular' was at last established and agreed.

Box 2 Basic principles for grand lodge recognition

1. Regularity of origin: every grand lodge must be established by a regular grand lodge.
2. Belief in the Great Architect of the Universe is a mandatory membership requirement.
3. All initiates take their oath on or in full view of the open Volume of the Sacred Law (no specific religion is mentioned here).
4. Membership is exclusively male. No intercourse is permitted with mixed lodges or with lodges admitting women.
5. Sovereign jurisdiction exists over the lodges working in the first three degrees. (This regulation indirectly points at a territorial principle.)
6. The 'Three Great Lights of Freemasonry' (i.e., the Square, Compasses, and Volume of the Sacred Law) must be displayed at lodge meetings.
7. Discussion of religion and politics within the lodge is prohibited.
8. The principles of the 'Antient Landmarks' shall be observed (although there is no clear definition of what these entail).

Another organizational principle that developed over the course of the centuries is that of 'territorial sovereignty'. This principle suggests that only one grand lodge can be recognized in any given territory. This rule has been particularly important for freemasonry in the USA, being imposed to avoid territorial arguments between grand lodges of the various states—despite several attempts to create a federal masonic body in the USA. However, African-Americans have developed their own system of freemasonry, called Prince Hall freemasonry, which has clearly fulfilled the criteria for regularity since its establishment in the 18th century. Since Prince Hall grand lodges in some states have also been recognized by fellow mainstream grand lodges in the same state, UGLE decided to do the same, although with some notable exceptions in the southern states.

With various grand lodges operating nationwide, the situation in Germany prior to 1935 was rather complex. In order to resolve this, after 1945, an umbrella grand lodge was inaugurated that now acts as the sole representative of German freemasonry on an international level, despite the existence of five independent and regular grand lodges, which preserved their own internatonal contacts. This demonstrates how, in some cases, regular and recognized grand lodges have maintained contact with irregular and unrecognized grand lodges.

Issues of recognition and regularity mostly affect relations between the UGLE and GODF forms of freemasonry. However, it must be stressed that the differences in masonic practice are extremely marginal. A GODF lodge meeting in Paris and a UGLE lodge meeting in London follow basically the same pattern, and members certainly have similar motives to join and find similar things attractive about membership. The documentary *Terra Masonica* (2016) by Belgian director Tristan Bourlard provides an impressive insight into the similarity and variety of masonic workings across the globe, regardless of how regular they are seen to be by each other.

In practical terms, the policies that have been in place since 1877/1929 mainly affect the possibility of 'inter-visitation'. The right of individual members to attend masonic lodges of other systems is restricted by grand lodge policies, and an unauthorized visit might result in exclusion from their own lodge or other disciplinary measures. However, despite these policies, mutual visits on an individual lodge level have often taken place.

More important than inter-visitation rights are the financial aspects and the rights over the masonic brand within a given territory. Although most of the income from membership fees is retained at the local lodge level, a considerable amount is transferred to the provincial and national grand lodges; principles of regularity and territorial sovereignty are seen as important in terms of attempting to avoid competition. However, this is an ongoing problem, since in many countries a number of masonic bodies do exist within a single territory and they do compete for the same pool of potential members, at least among those who are able to offer the higher degrees.

The reputational damage to organizations which are seen to be operating outside the framework of established masonic practices is difficult to estimate, but is definitely a key factor for preserving strict rules for regularity, even in non-UGLE recognized settings. For instance, one unrecognized masonic grand lodge is the self-styled 'Masonic High Council the Mother High Council, the World Governing Body of Craft Masonry'. This grand lodge formed in 2005, and, according to its website, runs lodges in most parts of the world—even, most strikingly, in the Middle East. A prominent example of a fake masonic association is the so-called 'Masonic Fraternal Police Department' (MFPD) in California, which made headlines in 2015. The MFPD claimed a history spanning three millennia with close ties to the Knights Templar; its leader was portrayed on social media wearing full masonic regalia.

On an international level, several attempts have been made to launch an overarching organization of freemasonry. A Bureau International de Relations Maçonniques existed between 1902 and 1921, followed by the Association Maçonique Internationale (which ceased its activities in 1950), and two further successors. Mixed gender and female only masonic organizations have their own international secretariats. Since 1995, the informal World Conference of Regular Masonic Grand Lodges gathers masonic leaders from across the globe.

A culture of self-governance

Margaret C. Jacob has stated that masonic lodges 'set up governments in microcosm, complete with elections, officers and taxes'. Lodges function as 'schools for government' and, more specifically, *democratic* government, involving complex forms of political organization. This culture of self-governance promotes a feeling of citizenship, with the right to participate in decision-making and governance. Within the lodges, freemasons throughout Europe and the world could experiment with and experience the benefits of parliamentarianism by voting, electing officers, collecting 'taxes', practising public oratory, settling disputes, and creating superordinate (national) bodies to which representatives were delegated. In terms of charitable work, the lodges offered help to the needy in an age when public/state welfare was unknown.

Well-kept archives of masonic bodies around the world are treasure troves for studying the material culture of the organization over three centuries. In many cases, grand lodges were the first central non-governmental organizations to exist on a national level, and as such they fostered both an imagined and a real consciousness of nationhood as a whole. On an international level, grand lodges created foreign alliances and treaties in a self-structured system of masonic diplomacy. As a precursor to the voluntary associations (and civil society) of later times, masonic national umbrella organizations were formed with regional and local nodes, national membership records, collection of fees, and rules for correspondence. In this sense, Jacob argues, members of the educated elites could experience important virtues of state formation, of a reformatory rather than revolutionary sort. These qualities were particularly relevant in regions where the fabric of state governance was virtually absent or still in genesis. This is particularly seen during the Western expansion into the USA, such as in California, in 1845–50, where masonic lodges created spaces of mutual assistance, impacting society building at the same time as promoting constitutional culture. The establishment of national grand lodges frequently preceded the formation of independent nation states.

On a more individual level, a good number of individual freemasons since the 18th century have been provided with masonic passports (so-called 'certificates'), allowing them entry to lodges across the globe and also granting access to benefits ('masonic relief') in foreign countries under certain circumstances. This social function of lodges became evident during the 19th-century mass migration from Europe to the USA. More importantly, it helped the members of masonic lodges to experience global solidarity in their practice.

Lodge organization, numbers, and names

The basic administrative unit and local node for all activities in freemasonry is the lodge, which is self-governed by officers elected from among its members and which follows its own by-laws. Apart from their symbolic roles in the enactment of ritual, these officers occupy designated functions in the administration of the lodge, such as master/chairman with deputies, treasurer, secretary, archivist, and so on (see Figure 6). From the early 1720s (at the latest), the grand lodge assumed the role of superior governing body with the right to regulate the activities of its subordinate lodges.

The Constitutions were approved by twenty individual lodges in 1723. By 1730, this number had multiplied to 160, according to *Masonry Dissected*. That list mentions a French lodge in London as well as lodges abroad, in cities such as Paris, Valenciennes, Aubigny, Lisbon, The Hague, Hamburg, Boston (MA), and Savannah (GA). From the outset, lodges as a rule did not choose their own names, but used those of the public and coffee houses (pubs) where they assembled. However, lodges did start to give themselves symbolic names such as 'friendship', 'fortitude', or 'cordiality' early on. From 1729 onwards, an engraved list of lodges was printed that displayed pub signs and meeting times. The impressive nine-volume publication, *Religious Ceremonies and Customs of All the Peoples of the World* (1723–43), included an article on freemasonry (volume 4, 1736). The article was illustrated with a grandiose display of the engraved lodge list as a background to one of the first images of modern freemasons

6. 'Le Tablier maçonnique' (1785).

assembled for a lodge meeting (see Figure 2). From this nucleus of roughly 160 lodges, thousands of lodges developed subsequently in Britain alone.

A standard work of reference is Lane's *Masonic Records* (1894), an authoritative listing of all lodges under the English masonic constitution from 1717 onward. This work has now been digitized and is fully searchable online. Lodges established after 1894 have also been added, and the highest serial number (as of 2012) is 9870. In the British case, praxis has evolved to allow the establishment of lodges that are smaller in membership size and that have specialized interests—frequently professional. This tradition started during the 18th century with the establishment of military or regimental lodges. On the continent, however, the pattern is rather different—the typical lodge tends to comprise members of all walks of life and has a rather high membership. Masonic lodge records thus provide interesting insights into biographies and social history, particularly in a colonial context. Famous lodges that gathered intellectuals together were established in Paris (Neuf Soeurs) and Vienna (Zur Eintracht). Proper research lodges came to life with the 1884 establishment of Quatuor Coronati No. 2076 in London (UGLE).

It is difficult to estimate the total number of members that have joined masonic lodges over the centuries. A digitized card index at the Bibliothèque nationale de France ('Fichier Bossu') has roughly 170,000 entries for the period 1780–1850. During the first century of Swedish Freemasonry (1737–1844), the number of members is calculated at roughly 15,000, and about the same number applies to Prussia and to Ulster (up to 1800). A prominent website for genealogical research has made English and Irish masonic membership registers from 1751 to 1921 available for research. No less than 1.7 million names are listed.

Chapter 7
Brotherhood challenged

From its outset, freemasonry was and still is perceived as a distinctly male form of sociability. However, criticism of its exclusion of women began early on and led to the establishment of female or mixed para-masonic orders and eventually to entirely female offshoots of mainstream freemasonry.

Medieval craft regulations allowed unmarried women to exercise trade on their own under the legal status of 'femme sole'. As a rule, this right was extended to widows of master craftsmen. Thus, it is possible to find women in building trades such as (free)masonry throughout history. In *The Book of the City of Ladies* (1405), a literary work by medieval author Christine de Pizane, women are depicted as actively engaged in masonry and in a host of other crafts. Pizane also introduced in her writings the figure of the Queen of Sheba or Balkis as a very positive intellectual female role model.

The exclusion of women from modern freemasonry was an invention of the 1723 publication, *The Constitutions*, which fuelled suspicions that masonic lodges were hotbeds of sodomy, a theme that has endured in anti-masonic lore ever since. Partly because of such external accusations, freemasonry developed strict rules for behaviour and did not hesitate to expel members who (potentially) brought lodges into disrepute. Freemasonry promoted and simultaneously limited the ideal of male friendship. Regarding religion, *The Constitutions* forbid atheism and agnosticism. The term 'irreligious libertine' is used to refer to atheism, a term that of course also has a carnal connotation—so that it simultaneously indicates the boundaries of religious (non-)belief and of proper sexual conduct. During the first two decades of freemasonry, the critique against its exclusion of women was mainly brought forward in articles and pamphlets. The first signs of real female participation occurred during the 1740s, other than some earlier exceptional cases. It was at this later point that the first female and mixed orders were created, modelled on the ritual pattern of regular freemasonry to form the first masonic 'lodges of adoption', as they were called. During the last decades of the 18th century, female freemasonry was being practised all over Europe.

The Enlightenment argued for both sexes to be treated similarly, based on the argument of shared universal rationality, a perspective that effectively led to a slowly increasing group of privileged women entering this associational world of men. A regression then occurred during the Romanticism era, when biological arguments of essential gender differences led to a stronger division between the sexes; consequently, female masonic affiliation levels dropped. However, at the end of the 19th century and the beginning of the 20th, in the generation that eventually brought women's suffrage and legal equality, a new surge of interest for female freemasonry manifested itself, also furthered by a re-evaluation of gender relations in certain strands of Western esotericism. In the century since then, feminism and ideas of gender equality have revived female participation in masonic lodges across the globe.

Organization and development of female freemasonry

The first signs of female participation in freemasonry are recorded as occurring in France in the 1740s. A contemporary French exposure on masonic rituals, *Le Parfait maçon*, shows striking similarities to the rituals later used in adoption freemasonry. Finally, in 1745, the publication *L'Ordre des Franc-Maçons trahi et le secret des Mopses revelée* revealed, besides those of freemasonry, the secrets of the mixed-gender Order of Mopses. Allegedly founded in Vienna in 1738, the Order of Mopses imitated masonic ceremonies with a focus on the pug dog as a symbol of trust, affection, and fidelity. No matter how ridiculous a modern reader may initially find the rituals of this order (which eventually spread across Europe), it allowed a larger group of women to partake in the enlightened associational world that was previously kept almost completely exclusive to men. Women could develop agency in ceremonial functions, engage in the formal organization of sociability, and assume administrative responsibility in a private zone that was free of ordinary conventions. To a certain degree, privileged women already participated in courtly (frequently Arcadian) role-playing enacted within the imagined realm of classical literature. For instance, a mixed-gender Order of Amaranth was established in 1653 at the court of Queen Christina in Stockholm. However, these relaxations of strict etiquette were only extended to a select few among the high aristocracy.

The Order of Abelites, founded in 1746, and the Anti-Masonic Society, established in 1739, had similarities in that both were mixed-gender, emerged in lower social strata in Pietism, and criticized freemasonry for its exclusion of women. The 'Order of Oculists', dating from the 1740s, argued similarly; their rituals were recently discovered in the 'Copiale' manuscript, written entirely in cipher. Swedish proto-feminist author Hedvig Charlotta Nordenflycht established her own mixed-gender 'Ordre de la Resemblance' in 1747, elaborating on the idea of equality and elective affinities among its members. Numerous other examples existed, demonstrating a considerable dynamic in mixed-gender or all-female sociability during the 18th century, promoted by the Enlightenment cult of emancipated friendship.

It is unclear whether the establishment of adoption freemasonry was in response to these earlier groups, but nonetheless from the mid-1760s onwards, well-composed rituals for female masonic lodges were being disseminated in manuscript and print form. Equally, there appeared to exist an affinity between those engaged in the dissemination of higher degrees and those involved in adoption freemasonry. In 1774, the GODF officially recognized adoption lodges and introduced standardized rituals, rules, and regulations for them. The word 'adoption' was originally used as a synonym for 'initiation', however in the new French model, female lodges were 'adopted' by male lodges; male freemasons were allowed to visit adoption lodges where most if not all offices were occupied by women.

Until the French Revolution, court nobility dominated membership in adoption freemasonry. Lodges were also established outside of France, but documentary evidence of a warrant by the GODF has only been found in Stockholm. On his mesmerizing travels through Europe, the infamous mystic Cagliostro founded a lodge of adoption in Courland at the Baltic Sea and initiated women into his own 'Egyptian rite'. Almost at the same time, the masonic Knights Templar of the Strict Observance discussed the establishment of a female branch. Their elaborate plan—which was, however, never implemented—outlines female freemasonry in five degrees. In the supreme degree, the female candidate wears a ceremonial hat, symbolizing that she must be prepared to defend the privileges of the order in times of trouble. Without exaggerating the importance of this element of the ritual, it indicated a crossing of traditional gender roles, albeit a symbolic one. Female higher degrees, such as the Amazonnerie Anglaise, were eventually developed in which women occupied central positions and ritually expressed their casting off of male dominance. The sisters were instructed to study sciences and to use arms. It is possible that the increased tolerance towards women in freemasonry influenced the composition of

Mozart's *The Magic Flute* (1791), where female characters play a crucial role in the musical initiation drama.

After a hiatus in masonic activities in France due to the French Revolution, adoption masonry was revived under the auspices of the Empress Joséphine, highlighting the general function of freemasonry as an element of bourgeois elite sociability in Napoleonic France (see Figure 7). In general, however, female participation in freemasonry declined in Europe throughout the 19th century. In contrast, a female masonic body was created in the USA in 1850, the still-existing Order of the Eastern Star, with about one million members worldwide. Several other female orders that are closely associated with freemasonry also exist. In Scandinavia and northern Germany, the secretive Order of Maria (established in 1917) contains around 7,000 members and has grown considerably over the last three decades. The Hermetic Order of the Golden Dawn, founded by three freemasons in Britain at the end of the 19th century, allowed both female and male membership, since masculinity and femininity were esoterically interpreted as two poles of a single unity. Similar orders were established in Denmark, Sweden, and northern Germany around 1800, demonstrating that the ideas circulating in Western esotericism at that time generally furthered gender equality.

The largest and most influential mixed masonic order was Le Droit Humain (DH), established in 1893 as a consequence of the initiation of feminist leader Maria Deraismes into a male lodge in Paris. DH worked (and still works) with the male rituals, and expanded its dissemination considerably with the initiation of theosophist, writer, and social activist Annie Besant in 1902. Over the course of fifteen years, Besant founded more than 400 lodges of DH throughout the world. The English-speaking lodges adopted a ritual that was more inspired by Besant's theosophical ideas than by traditional masonic teachings. In 2001, the British section of DH split into two factions over the issue of ritual conformity. An entirely female Grande Loge Féminine de France

7. 'La Loge d'adoption' (around 1824).

was established in 1945 and traces its origins back to 1901. Today, it is the largest all-female grand lodge in the world. At the outset, it worked with the 18th-century adoption ritual, but it changed in the late 1950s to a mainstream version of the male rituals. An Order of Women Freemasons was established in 1953 in Britain and the Frauen Großloge von Deutschland was established in Germany in 1982.

The female adoption ritual

One of the famous Jagiellonian Renaissance tapestries at Wawel Castle in Krakow, Poland, displays the construction of the Ark of Noah. Strikingly, not only are Noah's sons Shem, Ham, and Japhet portrayed working on the elaborate carpentry of the Ark, but also his daughters-in-law. Although their names are not mentioned in the Bible, these female carpenters were generally revered as the mothers of the post-diluvian human race; in some extra-biblical traditions, they were associated with female prophets and oracles. The Ark of Noah plays a central role in the female adoption ritual in freemasonry.

Anderson's *The Constitutions* claims that 'the GREAT ARK, [. . .] tho' of Wood, was certainly fabricated by GEOMETRY, and according to the Rules of MASONRY'. One of the first versions of the masonic third degree legend, the so-called Graham manuscript of 1726, replaces the Temple architect with Noah. It is therefore not far-fetched to talk about a Noachite tradition in freemasonry, in which the transmission of knowledge from ante- to post-diluvian humankind plays a central role. Carpentry, along with its biblical symbolism, was also transformed into a ritual motif in masonic-like fraternities such as that of the Order of Carpenters, allegedly founded in 16th-century England, which, since its later inception in 1761 in Sweden, is still flourishing today.

Female freemasonry was divided into three degrees: Apprentice, Fellow, and Master. Higher degrees were also developed. The ritual of the first degree unfolds in principle as it does in male freemasonry and is subsequently described in a typical late-18th-century variety. The candidate is prepared outside the lodge room and introduced blindfolded into the lodge. A tracing board displays Noah's Ark, the Tower of Babel, and a ladder with five rungs (the number five occupies a central symbolic role in female freemasonry). After walking around the room, the blindfold is released. The candidate catches sight of a 'terrifying brother', the 'Frère Terrible' with a flaming sword, symbolizing the Angel in Paradise. The candidate takes an oath of fidelity, receives the tokens of an apprentice, and is instructed in the teachings of her degree. The ceremony is concluded with a catechism in which, among many questions and answers, the central symbols of the degree are explained as follows:

Q: What does the Tower of Babel represent?
A: The arrogance of the children of this world, which one cannot sympathise with unless you have a selfish heart, and to cure it accordingly becomes the right token of a Freemason and a female Freemason.
Q: What does Jacob's Ladder signify?
A: This Ladder is full of secrets. Both sides of the Ladder represent the love for God and the love for the neighbour. And in between those sides, there are the virtues that originate from a noble soul.
Q: What does Noah's Ark signify?
A: The heart of the human being, which is carried and driven by its passions like the Ark by the water of the Flood.

The second degree, the Companion degree, revolves around the Garden of Eden, the stigmatization of Eve's eating of the apple from the Tree of Knowledge, and the subsequent expulsion from Paradise. The candidate is identified with Eve, but in a crucial scene of the ritual, she is told:

Here is the bite in the apple by the first human, there the death of the descendants; to diminish and mitigate this punishment, freemasonry is a necessary remedy: as the practice of every moral virtue teaches us to face this fatal moment with fortitude.

Then the candidate is brought 'from death to life' and is shown an eight-pointed burning star; she is told:

> Do you see, my Sister, this Eastern Star is the enlightenment of reason and the right light of masonry from which we do not depart because it is by [the star] we are led to true felicity.

The candidate then takes an oath for the second degree, performs the symbolic eating of the apple and sealing of her lips (with almond paste), and is dressed with new tokens of companionship. Two elements of the second degree catechism deserve particular attention. The companion is examined as follows:

Q: What do you think when you hear the difficult word Eve?
A: It leads me back to my origin and shows me what I am and what I should be, in remembrance of the highest felicity.

When asked about the word of the degree, the sister replies:

> Belba! Which means peace and unity, which—through the bringing down of the [Babylonian] Tower of disorder—has been restored among Brethren and Sisters as the prophecy of the Sibyls foretells.

The tracing board of the supreme degree of Mistress displays no less than nine scenes from the Old Testament: a rainbow, the sacrifice of Noah, and that of Abraham, Noah's Ark on Mount Ararat, the Babylonian tower, the burning of Sodom and Gomorrah, the transformation of Lot's wife into a salt pillar, the dream of Joseph, and finally Joseph in the well. Once the sister companion is brought in blindfolded, she is asked to climb a real 'mysterious Ladder' (mentioned in the first degree catechism). Supported by a sister, she finally arrives at the fifth and 'highest step of felicity [...] which many thousands strive to attain'.

Thereafter, she takes an oath and is brought to work: the symbolic centrepiece of the third degree ritual.

The candidate is asked to give five blows with different tools upon a wooden box. A secret mechanism opens the lid, and an illuminated heart rises up from the box. The master of the lodge asks the freemasons present: 'What has the sister brought forth?' and receives the reply, 'Worshipful Master, a heart has been brought out of it.' The ceremony is explained as freemasonry giving dominion over the heart and teaching how to make the 'most compassionate and tender out of the hardest and most relentless'. The catechism basically explains the tracing board and repeats the idea that the Ark symbolizes the 'human heart driven by passions'. To 'bring down the Tower of disorder' is yet another central aspect that is explained extensively:

Q: What other lessons does it teach us?
A: That without unity and understanding between one another, the love and friendship of the Society cannot last.
Q: How is understanding restored?
A: Through the peace and unity that can be seen to reign among Brethren and Sisters.

The ritual of adoption allows various possible interpretations. From a purely misogynistic understanding, it is all about reinforcing female guilt for the original sin. However, a more careful reading provides clues to a separate ritual identity being established, one that is intended to restore original innocence: 'the myth of Eden is confronted and the story reworked', as Margaret C. Jacob has convincingly argued. The candidate of the second degree is identified with Eve, yet her freemasonry has the potential to ease the burden placed on women. Her initiation offers a way out of mortality: the female companion is integrated into the 'enlightenment of reason' through illumination by the Eastern Star (which may have a Christian connotation, and may thus symbolize the initiate being embraced by divine grace).

Independently contemplating her origin, the female companion is empowered to develop a positive vision of herself for the future: the Babylonian confusion can be overcome, and peace and harmony can be restored, 'as the prophecy of the Sibyls foretells'.

The only clue given in the ritual that Noah's daughters-in-law appear in adoption masonry is in the Sibylline Oracles, a collection of classical, Christian, and esoteric writings in verse from the 6th or 7th century, where these women's names are given, and one of them (the 'Babylonian Sibyl') is identified as the mother of the Greek oracles.

Finally, by climbing a 'Ladder of Felicity', the female freemason reaches towards mastery. This is ultimately achieved by knocking on the mechanical chest, which displays a heart. The question is, what does this chest actually symbolize? Reading the catechisms of the degrees together makes it obvious that Noah's Ark is not only understood in its biblical sense, it also symbolizes the human heart carried away by its passions. Hidden inside this heart (represented by the chest), however, drifting randomly on the ocean of God's punishment, is yet another heart: the pure heart of compassion and tenderness. This second heart can only be released by an autonomous and conscious act, using the tools of masonry. On a symbolic level, the ritual suggests that in this way, not only can the Babylonian confusion be overcome, but also, potentially, the inequality between the sexes, since understanding is restored through peace and unity among brethren and sisters.

Compared with male freemasonry, the adoption ritual is no less performative or symbolic, and is therefore not a simplified version of the male equivalent. Its motifs are derived and fleshed out from direct and alternative readings of biblical stories. Some elements hint at the influence of higher degrees in male freemasonry; for instance, the candidate receives a wristband with the motto 'Silence and Virtue', an element that is also practised in the rituals of the Royal Order of Scotland of Heredom and Kilwinning. The mysterious ladder has a parallel to the second degree tracing board in male freemasonry (although that ladder has seven steps and symbolizes Jacob's Ladder), but more importantly it parallels the so-called 'Rosecroix of Heredom' (the eighteenth degree in AASR), a degree in which the Scottish master and the Royal Arch are about to find and restore the lost Word. At first sight, the rituals appear to be a 'feminized' version of the male ritual, however, theoretically, they could have been used independently as separate higher degrees.

It is tempting to speculate on the impact the adoption ritual had upon women of the 18th and 19th centuries. What happened when they learned that original sin could be overcome (or at least mitigated) and that they as sisters could share illumination by reason on equal terms with their masonic brothers? Jan Snoek, who has researched rituals of adoption extensively, interprets the rituals from the perspective of 'felix culpa' ('happy guilt'). In these rituals, Eve can be likened to Christ. By taking the burden of sin upon herself, Eve opens the door to the experience of felicity during our lifetimes, enabling us to choose what is right and virtuous, in our new knowledge of alternatives.

As in the male masonic third degree, the candidate in the second degree of the adoption ritual is thus identified with a deity. According to the ritual, true felicity is achieved when this identification is done in community, establishing an understanding between men and women in the elective affinity between sisters and brothers in freemasonry. Although only embraced by a relatively small number of women, adoption freemasonry has been seen as a form of early feminism, a 'female rite of passage into the culture of the Enlightenment'.

Chapter 8
Perceptions, prejudices, and persecutions

Starting with early negative treatment in the press in the 18th century, freemasonry became an object of public persecution by governmental and Church authorities across Europe—persecution that peaked with the first papal ban in 1738 (the first of many). However, the brotherhood was first seriously exposed to governmental investigation when freemasonry was alleged to have contributed to the French Revolution in widespread political conspiracy theories. As a result, the Unlawful Societies Act was passed in 1799 by the British parliament, and was followed by restrictions and prohibitions in a number of other European countries. In the USA, an Anti-Masonic Party formed during the 1820s, fuelled by anti-masonic discourse in Europe. In Catholic and Orthodox countries, freemasonry was forced into secrecy due to predominantly religious prohibition, persecution, and accusations of 'Satanism'. This tendency towards secrecy deepened in these countries to protect freemasonry, which was frequently featured in liberal, national, and secular elite sociability.

At the turn of the 20th century, anti-masonic ideas were blended with anti-Semitic conspiracy theories such as the Russian Tsarist forgery, Protocols of the Elders of Zion. Anti-masonic ideas were then included in fantasies of a secret 'world conspiracy', as formulated in Nazi imagination after the German defeat in

World War I. Fascist rulers in Europe suppressed freemasonry, confiscated lodge property, and persecuted individual freemasons. The same pattern was repeated in the totalitarian communist systems of Eastern Europe. Although freemasonry had initially thrived, during the first 'Nahda', the spiritual awakening of Arab nationalism during the late 19th and early 20th centuries, in the Middle East it has since been prohibited, its members persecuted, and included in virulent anti-Western conspiracy theories. Today, conspiracy narratives about freemasonry (and secret societies in general) are widely disseminated via the Internet and in pop culture references. Theories about a presumed plutocratic 'new world order' (NWO) have re-emerged during the late 20th century, reinforcing the idea that our lives are governed by secret elites who orchestrate cover-ups of the 'truth'.

Freemasonry and the press—topics and trends

From the very moment modern freemasonry entered the associational world of early 18th-century London, it featured in the urban press. No less than 12,000 references relating to freemasonry were found in the British press between 1709 and 1813. The sheer number of press references shows just how visible and public freemasonry actually was during that period: with that level of notoriety, freemasonry could hardly be called secret.

Nonetheless, the issue of secrets and secrecy in freemasonry was (and is) among the most prominent in relation to the fraternity that have been addressed in the press. Secret signs, words, places, modes of recognition, and rituals fire the imagination of those in the media, and their audience, the former clearly prospering from the topic. Negative focus has also been on the concept of members taking the masonic oath. Aside from religious objections, it has been argued that taking an oath in a private association undermines one's loyalty to the State authorities. Criticism of the masonic oath only deepened with the revelation of the penalties attached by the fraternity to breaking this oath—torture and capital punishment—even when freemasons assured the public that these penalties were only to be understood on a symbolic level.

The exclusion of women flamed suspicion that freemasons were engaged in sodomy. Masonic conviviality was denounced as a bacchanalian excess of intemperance and gluttony, and membership was denigrated as fraudulent and immoral moneymaking on behalf of the lodges. The fraternity's social exclusivity as well as their bridging of different social strata were also questioned, particularly during the 18th century when social equality was an issue. Despite its fraternal egalitarianism on the level of ideas, freemasonry retained an aura of elite sociability, which nurtured the perception of there being a close affiliation between the fraternity and other influential groups in society that were in positions of political or economic power.

On a positive note, freemasons were seen to be openly engaged in cultural life, regularly visiting theatre performances and readings of various masonic prologues or poems. Masonic processions publicly displayed both their members and their symbols. Charitable projects in the wider community, which were often of a novel and ground-breaking character, were reported on extensively. Masonic sociability was publicized in different ways and thus promoted the success of the fraternity as a visible feature of British mainstream culture. The press and the fraternity developed a mutually beneficial relationship since reporting on freemasonry led to enhanced circulation of media publications while expanding advertising revenue. However, as discussed earlier, despite these public appearances that promoted a sense of transparency, freemasonry was not exempt from criticism and ridicule. In 1741–2, a mock masonic procession called the 'Scald Miserable Masons' was enacted in London and images of it were disseminated in print. Hogarth captured the anti-masonic irony of the period in some of his prints, most notably 'Night' and 'The Mystery of Masonry brought to Light by the Gormogons'.

The 'Gormogons' was the first anti-masonic fraternity (among several to follow); it was established in the 1720s by disillusioned masons, imitating and mocking the form and content of freemasonry. The presumed antiquity of the craft and its mysteries were frequently derided. Throughout the history of freemasonry, schisms or the formation of pseudo-masonic bodies—from the Gormogons to the secret Italian lodge, Propaganda Due—have generated publicity and attention, circulating sensational revelations in all forms of media. Starting with the printing of parts of the masonic catechism in the press and with *Masonry Dissected* (1730), the first full-text publication of the ritual (with at least thirty editions up to 1800 and translations into most other European languages), exposure literature became an integral feature of media coverage.

The most momentous association, however, was that between freemasonry and politics. The tone of *The Constitutions* and the patronage and membership of 18th-century English freemasonry already placed it close to the new Hanoverian dynasty. The press expanded its coverage of freemasonry, especially after the first governmental oppressions in European cities such as Florence, The Hague, Bern, and Paris, culminating with the first papal condemnation of freemasonry in 1738. A steady stream of vindications of freemasonry appeared in print in the period immediately after the papal condemnation. By the end of the 1730s, freemasonry had emerged as a transnational media topic in the periodical press in Europe and beyond. Yet another peak of transnational media coverage then occurred in the aftermath of the exposure, *L'Ordre des Franc-maçons trahi* (1745), a publication that was immediately translated into a number of languages. *L'Ordre* also marked the start of a dynamic period of print outlets such as handbooks, pocket companions, almanacs, anthologies of orations, songbooks, and so on, primarily produced for a masonic target audience. In many cases, a significant reason for these publications was a bid to counterbalance false rumours and negative publicity; however, it is clear that the growing (and rather privileged) membership of masonic lodges across Europe was creating a demand for specialized reading as well as news coverage.

The first major journals entirely dedicated to a masonic reading public were the *Journal für Freymaurer*, appearing in no fewer than twelve volumes between 1784 and 1786 in Vienna, and the *Freemasons' Magazine*, published in London between 1793 and 1799. The *Journal* was issued in 1,000 copies and distributed across the vast territory of the Habsburg Empire. The establishment of the *Journal* must be seen against the backdrop of almost unprecedented news coverage of freemasonry in the German press during the 1780s and 1790s. More than 100 articles on this topic, totalling more than 1,200 pages of print, appeared in German periodicals of the Enlightenment period, with a clear peak in readership during the immediate pre-Revolution era. The *Freemasons' Magazine* appeared in eleven volumes between 1793 and 1798 (slightly preceded by the *Sentimental and Masonic Magazine*, published in Dublin between 1792 and 1795). In 1797, it was renamed the *Scientific Magazine*.

This magazine can be regarded as an archetype of later masonic periodicals, which further evolved into a veritable masonic press by the middle of the 19th century; and some of these periodicals survived well into the 20th century. During the first century of their existence, masonic periodicals took part in the on-going debates and controversies surrounding freemasonry in the culture and society of their time; however, in due course they turned their focus more on purely internal issues, attempting little connection with the outside world.

Ramsay's 'Discours' linked freemasonry to the chivalric orders of the Crusades, which predominantly influenced the internal development of freemasonry between 1740 and 1780. In the 1780s, however, in connection with the collapse of the Knights Templar rite of the 'Strict Observance' (1782) and the discovery and prohibition of the Bavarian 'Illuminati' (1785), anti-masonic arguments assumed a considerably more ideological character. A sinister twist was introduced into the anti-masonic narrative, focusing on presumed plots by secret forces, either in support of radical Enlightenment groups or its irrational opponents. The subject was complex and contradictory. In some cases, the Templar element was used as an indication of secret Jesuit machinations, explaining why these forms of freemasonry were branded as 'crypto-Catholic'. In other cases, the Templar myth was assigned a political meaning, since the French Revolution could be interpreted as a 'revenge' against the French monarchy and Church. Illuminati infiltration of masonic lodges (whether true or imagined) provided so-called proof that freemasonry was not immune to exploitation for political purposes, and that an initiated hierarchy of 'unknown superiors' was secretly pulling the strings of other members who had been kept in a state of ignorance.

The American Declaration of Independence (1776) was generally met with enthusiasm or at least with compassion by members of the educated European elites. Nevertheless, the events of the French Revolution—the execution of the royal couple, the introduction of uncompromising secular republicanism paired with a universal declaration of human rights, and, finally, the reign of terror—challenged the tolerance of the general public and profoundly alarmed sovereigns across the continent. In the fevered search for culprits that followed the Revolution, it was only a matter of time before intense focus was directed on secret societies in general and on freemasonry in particular. The bottom line of the conspiracy argument was that freemasonry represented one of the radical Enlightenment forces that undermined traditional authority—both secular and sacred.

Regulation and suppression

Over the centuries, secular and sacred authorities alike have raised concerns about the existence of masonic lodges. As a general tendency throughout history, the more authoritarian a political system, the more freemasonry has been persecuted within it. Before the French Revolution, freemasonry was condemned by the Vatican and by Protestant clergy (particularly Pietistic clergy, or what would be called evangelical leaders today); it was also suppressed by a number of secular authorities. However, these condemnations and suppressions did not prevent the global dissemination of freemasonry.

The reasons for the issuing of the first papal bull against masonic gatherings, entitled *In Eminenti* (March 1738), are complex. The bull stated that an association of persons belonging to different faiths was in itself heretical and that the practice of freemasonry furthered depraved behaviour; this lead to bans in several countries. Furthermore, the bull attacked the misuse of the masonic oath of secrecy: if freemasonry was not intended to be in contravention of religion and the State, why then did it contain secrets? However, the most imprecise reason for the bull was given as 'other just and reasonable motives', which were (presumably) known only to the Holy See itself.

At this particular time, freemasonry in France was divided into two camps: lodges that had been established by the grand lodge of England, which was Hanoverian in its political allegiance, and lodges established by Jacobites, who supported the succession of the ousted Stuart monarchy to the British throne. In the aftermath of the papal bull, Parisian police authorities carried out investigations and spectacular raids on masonic lodges; indeed it has been suggested that the papal ban supported domestic politics in France at that time. However, the bull didn't ever achieve legal status in France, hinting at a general crisis of papal authority in the 18th century. In Italy, freemasonry was identified as a source of threat in Florence where the lodge included anti-clerical freethinkers, unlike the Catholic Jacobite freemasons of Rome. As such, it is possible that the real reasons for the Vatican's condemnation of freemasonry were most strongly linked to domestic Vatican and Italian politics of the time: distinct, local, personal issues as opposed to general, ideological factors.

Nevertheless, the papal ban received widespread attention across Europe, in effect simply furthering wider public knowledge and awareness of freemasonry. Indeed, when in the aftermath of *In Eminenti*, a pamphlet entitled *Relation Apologique et Historique de la Société des Franc-Maçons*, which defended freemasonry, was put on the infamous 'Index of Prohibited Works' and then burnt at the stake in Rome in February 1739, the news spread as far as Boston in America. Since this booklet of about ninety pages was the only publication on freemasonry that had experienced such a fate, it deserves a short introduction. The *Relation* appeared under a false imprint (Dublin) during the spring of 1738 and again as a series of articles in a widely read political journal published in Luxemburg, in the Austrian Netherlands; and by August of the same year, significant parts of the booklet had been translated into German and Swedish.

The pamphlet closely associated freemasonry with the Newtonian scientific culture of the period in general, and with the pantheist worldviews of the freethinker and philosopher John Toland in particular. It described masonic lodges as learned academies that engaged in research and philosophical investigation of the deep mysteries of nature. Refuting exposures by the Parisian police authority that had been published in 1737, the author presented a version of masonic ritual that has no resemblance to any known practices at the time. This brings the authorship into question, as well as the intentions of the pamphlet; even more, it invites the question of how the pamphlet came to the attention of the papal authorities and why they treated it as heretic and deserving of incineration. Clearly, however, this episode demonstrates that freemasonry—at least when it was identified with pantheism and Newtonian science—was perceived as representing an ideological threat.

In 1751, the papal ban was renewed under the title *Providas*. Again, the complex political context of Italian freemasonry (in Florence and Rome) must be taken into consideration, along with the circulation at this time of an anti-masonic tract that was even included in one of the first Italian encyclopaedias. *Providas* went even further than the previous bull, stating clearly (with references to Roman law) that associations formed without the permission of public authorities were illegal. In 1786, possibly spurred by a contemporary intensification of anti-masonic writings, the original bull, *In Eminenti*, was re-issued.

Nonetheless, despite these attempts to prevent the spread of freemasonry, tens of thousands of Catholics—even clerics—joined masonic lodges throughout the 18th century.

The Vatican obsession with freemasonry intensified considerably during the 19th century, fired by the vague insinuation by the Holy See that it was in possession 'of just and reasonable motives' for its condemnation. Particularly in Latin Europe, the USA, and South America, freemasonry was accused of conspiring against Church and State; between 1821 and 1884, it was condemned by the Holy See on a number of occasions. After 1884, the Catholic Church engaged in an intense propaganda war against freemasonry. Anti-masonic associations and magazines were created and congresses were held, which in turn reinforced the anti-clericalism of (predominantly Latin) freemasonry. While this was going on, political societies fighting for the unification of Italy were adopting overtly anti-clerical and secularist agendas, inspired by the then current French ideology of 'laïcité': a strict separation of religion and political life. Apart from the inherent ideological antagonism of the Catholic Church towards freemasonry, all this activism must be interpreted against the backdrop of its loss of secular power due to Italian unification, evident in the politics of the time. Indeed, since Vatican II (1962–5), the relationship between the Catholic Church and freemasonry has eased, having at least been discussed on a number of occasions. However, it does remain an uneasy one to this day as the recent row on the Order of the Knights of Malta forcefully demonstrates, accused of being undermined by freemasons.

After the French Revolution, a steady stream of conspiracy literature prepared the ground for governmental regulation of freemasonry across Europe. Masonic lodges more or less voluntarily ceased to operate in the Austrian and Russian empires. Prussia passed legislation against secret societies in 1798, as did Britain in 1799 and Sweden in 1803. In these surprisingly similar regulations, freemasonry was exempted from outright prohibition, but it was placed under governmental control. These regulations state that secrecy in general as well as private oaths of allegiance (in particular to 'unknown superiors') threaten the security of the State, and that meetings at which political and social issues are to be discussed are seditious as a matter of principle. Thus, at the turn of the 19th century, the voluntary association of citizens within freemasonry and similar fraternal orders was seen as posing a problem to governments across Europe. In Russia, secret societies (including freemasonry) were completely banned in 1822.

The modern conspiracy myth

The first modern conspiracy myth was born in connection with the French Revolution: it insinuated that political events had been triggered and deliberately orchestrated by dark forces that were opposed to Crown and Church and, ultimately, opposed to humankind. This idea was furthered by the writings of the Jesuit Augustin Barruel, who published the four-volume work *Mémoires pour servir à l'histoire du Jacobinisme* (1797–8) during his time of exile in London. Barruel accused anti-Christian Enlightenment philosophy of undermining the old order of Crown and Church. According to Barruel, freemasonry furthered this development by promoting freedom and equality. Finally, he held that the Illuminati—with their supposedly anarchist and Satanist spirit—were directly responsible for the Revolution. In the final volume of his work, he linked all these groups back to major heresies in world history.

At nearly the same juncture, John Robison, an Edinburgh professor of natural philosophy, also accused the Illuminati of being the main perpetrator of the French Revolution in his famous *Proofs of a Conspiracy against all the Religions and Governments of Europe, carried on in the secret meetings of Freemasons, Illuminati and Reading Societies* (1797). Once this myth was established, it was impossible to pull it back. Fuelled by conspiracy literature and spectacular press accounts, the 'proofs of a conspiracy' became a commonplace in public perception, and were adopted by increasingly suspicious and nervous conservative governments in a clampdown on voluntary associations. Governmental regulations and prohibitions codified distrust and scapegoating across Europe. In the USA, conservative clerics gripped by Illuminati-related panic accused Thomas Jefferson, one of the first US presidents, of being a representative of the Order. About three decades later, the Anti-Masonic Party was established in the aftermath of the Morgan Affair, where a printer was alleged to have been killed for threatening to publish a comprehensive exposure of American masonic rituals. For more than twenty years afterwards, public confidence in the fraternity was profoundly disturbed.

Freemasonry and anti-Semitism

However, the worst and most infamous conspiracy myth was yet to come. Occasioned by severe tensions in French society, where the particularly secularist ideology of 'laïcité' was colliding with that of the Church, Catholic anti-masonic feeling increased both on an organizational level and in content. The Vatican attacked freemasonry in a string of condemnations, with increasingly graphic accusations, such as of Satanism, sodomy, and sexual excesses. The papal encyclical *Humanum*

Genus (1884) divides the world into two camps: one influenced by the divine; the other, Satanic. This described freemasonry as a 'partisan of Evil'. Drawing upon these accusations, a French anti-clerical and atheist writer, Léo Taxil, invented a hoax: an account of Satanic freemasonry (venerating the diabolical figure of Baphomet, who he alleged was revered by the Templars); the intention was to mock both the brotherhood and Roman-Catholic opposition to it.

At around the same time, the Russian Tsarist secret service concocted the most toxic, anti-Semitic publication of modern times—the infamous *Protocols of the Elders of Zion*, which forecast a Judeo-masonic plot for world dominance. Barruel (mentioned earlier) had been contacted in 1806 by an Italian officer named Simonini, who encouraged him to publish an anti-Semitic sequel to his work. (The Italian novelist and intellectual historian Umberto Eco has outlined this feverish development in his novel *The Prague Cemetery* (2010), in a masterly mix of fact and fiction.) The *Protocols of the Elders of Zion* depicted freemasonry as a puppet of Judaism in a bid to achieve world dominance. All this demonstrated just how closely linked anti-masonic and anti-Semitic feelings were, and explains something of why the former was consequently suppressed by totalitarian fascist and socialist regimes alike (see Figure 8).

In 1919, the propagandist Friedrich Wichtl published *Weltfreimaurerei, Weltrevolution, Weltrepublik*, blaming Jews and freemasons alike for the outbreak of World War I. Wichtl's writings were immensely influential in setting the anti-Semitic agenda of the future National Socialist Party. Wichtl claimed that all major shifts in world politics since the French Revolution had been the result of a Judeo-masonic plot for world dominance. These ideas were picked up by a General Ludendorff, whose strategic miscalculations had ultimately contributed to the collapse of German warfare in World War I. He published *Vernichtung der*

8. 'L'Oeuvre de la Franc Maçonnerie. Révolution. Anarchie'.

Freimaurerei durch Enthüllung ihrer Geheimnisse—the 'elimination of freemasonry through revelation of its secrets'—in 1927. Finally, Alfred Rosenberg, the chief Nazi propagandist, repeatedly exploited anti-masonic and anti-Semitic conspiracy myths and thus laid the ideological foundation for the Holocaust.

The suppression of freemasonry under the Nazi regime and throughout the territories under Nazi occupation was based on these writings. In France, for instance, the main executive of this project of suppression, Bernard Faÿ, was also engaged in producing the first anti-masonic movie, *Forces Occultes* (1943; see Figure 1). The movie accused Jews and freemasons of having dragged the French Republic into war with Nazi Germany. *Forces Occultes* tells the story of a young member of parliament, Pierre Avenel, who is talked into joining a masonic lodge mainly for the purpose of career promotion. Major parts of the movie focus on details of his initiation ritual. In due course, Avenel is disillusioned with freemasonry, which he identifies as a tool of corruption and nepotism. As political tensions grow in French society and in French parliament, he realizes that the brotherhood constitutes a state within the State that is manipulating governmental decisions, encouraging warmongering, and essentially encouraging the destruction of law and order.

References to the masonic conspiracy myth in pop culture

The plot of Dan Brown's bestselling novel *The Lost Symbol* (2009) centres on a potential revelation that male representatives of the highest echelons of American legislative, judicial, and executive power have been caught on video, deeply involved in the performance of a masonic ritual. In the story, this potential revelation represents a serious threat to the national security of the United States, and must be prevented at any cost. It is felt that American society—much less the political allies and foes of this, as the story goes, last superpower and model of democracy—would never accept the engagement of these high-level representatives in the activities of a secret brotherhood; that the average citizen would be too ignorant to understand the fraternity and even less able to tolerate it. Hence, the most powerful unit in the American security services is sent to find and eliminate the main character, Mal'akh, who is threatening to release the incriminating video and, in his quest to gain the ultimate symbols of masonry, leaving a seemingly endless path of death and destruction behind him.

Luckily, symbologist Robert Langdon is also racing to prevent Mal'akh from further evil. Langdon deciphers the clues that lead him through the 'secret' architecture of the US capital, Washington, DC, right to the headquarters of an international masonic organization, the AASR (SJ 33°). On the altar of the organization's main temple, Mal'akh dies just seconds before the video is uploaded and e-mailed to some of the world's most prominent news agencies. Thus, the ultimate exposure of freemasonry in the 'fourth power'—the media—and the national disaster potentially emanating from such an exposure are prevented.

Dan Brown's novel is fiction, but it draws on common perceptions of freemasonry and its relationship to politics without which the plot would never have been exciting enough to create the tension that it did. These common perceptions are frequently exploited in popular culture across the globe and make up an increasing amount of the information on freemasonry that is available on the Internet, especially on sites such as YouTube.

If the Dan Brown novel exploited the still very strongly held conspiracy myth, the opposite perspective, one of ironic transformation, infused an episode of *The Simpsons* that was aired in 1995 and entitled 'Homer the Great'. Homer Simpson becomes a member of a secret society in Springfield, the 'Stonecutters', which has obvious similarities with freemasonry. Two of Homer's co-workers at the Springfield Nuclear Power Plant enjoy inexplicable privileges. He discovers that they are members of a secret fraternity that assembles at a vast temple with an all-seeing eye. Since he fulfils the membership criteria, Homer joins the fraternity; he is blindfolded, tested, and swears an oath of allegiance. After becoming a member, he enjoys preferential treatment by a craftsman, bypasses a traffic queue through a secret tunnel, and gets a more comfortable chair at his workplace. Gathered around the festive table of the Stonecutters, the members of the lodge (one of them a space alien) drink beer and sing the programmatic and catchy song of their fraternity. The lyrics elaborate typical motifs of conspiracy narratives that are spread widely on the Internet today—some, funnily enough, simply invented by the scriptwriters of *The Simpsons*. Thus we learn that the Stonecutters control the British pound/Crown, create movie stars, and rig every Oscar night; that they hold back the metric system and the electric car, rob cavefish of their sight, keep Atlantis off the maps, and conceal the existence of Martians.

For all its irony and humour, the Stonecutters episode draws upon a conspiracy culture that has since become an integral feature of fact-resistant world explanations that are reinforced by fringe radio, talk shows, websites, YouTube channels, and pop culture itself. Search results for the terms 'freemasonry' or 'Illuminati' show more than fifteen million hits, hinting at the prominence of these subjects in the thoughts of the general public. A veritable craze has developed for supposedly masonic or Illuminati imagery, which are assembled by conspiracy theorists as proof that the pop culture media is using the symbols to control the mind-sets of millions of people.

The attractiveness of the myth

From the outset, public perception of freemasonry was determined by a tension between secrecy and transparency, and the same tension remains today. In freemasonry, secrecy is a constitutive organizational feature and a key element of internal knowledge formation; thus, it is opposed to revelation, and revealing secrets/hidden material is and always has been one of the main purposes of all forms of news media outlets, from 18th-century journals to the Internet. It is therefore no wonder that freemasonry has always featured extensively in the press.

In addition, secrecy prompts speculation and prejudice, no matter how transparent freemasonry has generally been historically or today. The circularity of negative press treatment of freemasonry leading to apologetic writings by masonic representatives has created a dynamic that has prevailed throughout the centuries.

The standard objection voiced against masonic secrets is: how can the public trust what freemasonry says of itself, if secrecy is part of the masonic practice for initiates? How can initiates of lower degrees trust the aims and motives of their (potentially unknown) superiors? In the end, these questions cannot be answered in an entirely rational fashion. They are intimately connected to perceptions, anxieties, and the amount of mutual trust people are prepared to allow in interpersonal relations and society; in particular, they relate to how much trust governments are prepared to have in their citizens.

The popular association of freemasonry with conspiracy is partly due to the extraordinary claims the fraternity has made regarding its ancestry and importance, which have been a continual part of masonic lore. After all, *The Constitutions* associate freemasonry with almost all important building projects since the Ark. Ramsay's 'Discours' linked the fraternity to the medieval orders of the Crusades and (along with many later authors) to a host of ancient cults. Thus, the supposed connection between freemasonry and grandiose events and players in world history could easily be perceived as demonstrating the group's motivation to play a leading role in high-level, political events; and, as such, it is unsurprising if this has led to a recycling of these links in literature and pop culture references.

For more than three centuries, a link between freemasonry and political order has been part of many countries' public perception. People have imagined the secrecy of freemasonry as running contrary to the foundations of society under a variety of political systems, ranging from oppressive *anciens régimes* to totalitarian states and open democracies.

Through its organizational practices, freemasonry itself has indeed contributed to the development of political culture in civic society. The 'Great Schism' of 1877 introduced a division between masonic bodies with regards to societal and political activism. Masonic modes of organization could potentially be misused for the promotion of agendas of radical political change, as demonstrated by the Illuminati, some nationalistic, quasi-masonic associations such as the Italian 'Carbonari', and radical Irish loyalist orders. In other cases freemasonry has been closely aligned with the governing elites and an integral part of political culture. Adjustment of the politics of the time to the existence of freemasonry has either been smooth, as in the Scandinavian countries, or it has led to tensions with other groups in society, as in France.

The anti-masonic discourse of the 18th century, which has remained in latent existence since the beginnings of modern organized freemasonry in London, peaked around the time of the French Revolution. Freemasonry was seen not only as a danger to existing social order but also as potentially orchestrating radical political change. During the 19th and early 20th centuries, this perception opened the way for a mixing of anti-masonic sentiment with that of anti-Semitism and anti-socialism/communism. Equally, totalitarian communist regimes such as that of the Soviet Union also used anti-masonic thinking—only there freemasonry embodied the preservation of bourgeois political values (threatening those of a socialist/communist system) and had to be combated at any price. Prohibition of freemasonry and active persecution of masons then prevailed until the fall of the Berlin Wall.

The Home Affairs Committee investigations into the role of freemasonry in the judiciary and public life carried out in Britain around 2000 demonstrate that even in one of the oldest democracies of the world, perceptions of freemasonry continue to be uneasy. From the margins of public debate, the issue of freemasonry has moved into mainstream media and governmental decision-making processes, where stereotyped images have been recycled, images that are likely to remain for the foreseeable future. What is most remarkable is that the governmental inquiry and other groups have frequently stated that fears, negative publicity, public concerns, suspicions, allegations, perceptions, images and—perhaps most intriguing—'beliefs' are factors that must all be seriously taken into account in the political climate of the late 20th and early 21st centuries. This statement might be interpreted as indicating that the rules of public debate have been derailed, that arguments of passion are now placed above those of rational deliberation—and this has chilling parallels to the debates during 2016 surrounding Brexit and the US presidential election and the contemporary rise of populism in world politics.

It is not difficult to identify similarities between the current (post-)political climate and the weak democracies of the 1920s, when the proponents of totalitarian ideologies cunningly exploited purely emotional perceptions of political realities for their own purposes. Another interesting aspect of the British case from the late 1990s is that religious arguments against freemasonry were voiced (although not included in the governmental investigations). This seems to indicate that religion once again plays an increasingly important role in societal debates, even in open societies such as Britain. In the Catholic and Orthodox countries of Eastern Europe, freemasonry's alleged incompatibility with Christianity has re-emerged as one of its most noted features.

In the 21st century, religion has indeed returned as a strong factor in politics. In the contemporary climate of growing political polarization charged with religious undertones, it is not unlikely that a negative perception of freemasonry could soon be amalgamated with a politicized Islamophobia, both because of masonic religious tolerance and because of a naïve and inaccurate view that anything that might be branded anti-Christian or heterodox runs contrary to allegedly 'true' Western values. At the same time, freemasonry is an easy target for fundamentalist Islamism, which has incorporated and never revised anti-masonic conspiracy theories from the *Protocols of the Elders of Zion* discussed earlier. Such developments would follow the logics of both post-Revolutionary France and late-19th-century argumentation, but—more frighteningly—would be reminiscent of the situation in the 1920s, when freemasonry and its perceived role in world politics were demonized by both the far left and the far right.

Timeline

1717	Alleged founding date of the Grand Lodge of London and Westminster, the 'Moderns'.
1723	Publication of *The Constitutions*.
1730	Publication of *Masonry Dissected*, the first exposure on masonic ritual.
1736	Ramsay's 'Discours' links freemasonry to Chivalric orders of the Crusades. Between 1740 and 1760, a number of Chivalric degree systems in freemasonry are developed, most prominent being the 'Strict Observance' (1751–82).
1738	First papal condemnation, *In Eminenti*.
1745	Publication of *L'Ordre des Franc-maçons trahi*, first full-text (and visual) exposure, which also contains mention of the female quasi-masonic Order of Mopses.
1751	Foundation of the 'Antients' grand lodge.
1772	Foundation of the Grand Orient de France (GODF).
1770s	First female lodges that are fully accepted.
1790s	Conspiracy literature targets freemasonry as precursor of revolutionary and violent political change, which leads to governmental prohibitions and regulations.
1813	Union of the two English grand lodges, 'Antients' and 'Moderns', to form the United Grand Lodge of England and Wales (UGLE).
1820s–80s	Intensified papal condemnation of and Catholic agitation against freemasonry.

1822	Prohibition of freemasonry in Russia.
1826	The so-called 'Morgan Affair' unleashes two decades of anti-masonic sentiment in the USA (Anti-Masonic Party 1828–38).
1877	The GODF leaves it to its individual members' consciences to decide whether or not to take an oath on the Great Architect of the Universe, which causes a schism in international freemasonry.
1893	'Le Droit Humain', a mixed gender masonic order, is founded in Paris.
1903	Publication of the *Protocols of the Elders of Zion*, targeting freemasonry as a tool for alleged Jewish world dominance.
1929	Principles of grand lodge recognition agreed by UGLE cementing the schism in international freemasonry.
1920s–40s	Wave of anti-masonic feeling in European totalitarian states and intensified persecution during Nazi rule and occupation. Prohibition in place in Eastern Europe until 1989.
1990s	Political change in Europe leads to re-establishment of freemasonry in Eastern Europe and restitution of seized source material.
1997–9	Publication of two British Home Affairs Committee reports on freemasonry.
2010	The GODF accepts female members.
2000–16	Renewed scholarly interest in freemasonry.

Further reading

General reading

Titles listed here have been used throughout this book and have not necessarily been referenced explicitly within the text. For readers who want to explore the topics addressed in this book in greater depth, the following titles can be recommended:

Henrik Bogdan and Jan A.M. Snoek (eds), *Handbook of Freemasonry* (Brill, 2014).

Pierre-Yves Beaurepaire (ed.), *Dictionnaire de la franc-maçonnerie* (Armand Colin, 2014).

Róbert Péter (ed.), *British Freemasonry 1717–1813* (Routledge, 2016). A five-volume source collection with rare documents together with commentaries and introductions.

Pierre Mollier, Sylvie Bourel, and Laurent Portes, *La Franc-maçonnerie* (BNF, 2016). The catalogue of an exhibition organized at the Bibliothèque nationale de France in 2016.

Charles Porset and Cécile Révauger (eds), *Le Monde maçonnique des Lumières, Europe Amériques Colonies* (Champion, 2013). A three-volume biographical dictionary of 18th- and early-19th-century freemasons in Europe and the Americas with contributions from 150 authors.

Three academic journals are published in the field: IF—*Zeitschrift für Internationale Freimaurerforschung* (German and English, Studienverlag, hardback, since 1998); JRFF—*Journal for Research into Freemasonry and Fraternalism* (English and French, Equinox, hardback and electronic, since 2010); and REHMLAC—*Revista de Estudios Históricos de la Masonería Latinoamericana et Caribeña*

(Spanish, French, English, Universidad de Costa Rica, open access, since 2009).

The most comprehensive collection of masonic scholarship is gathered in the volumes of the UGLE research lodge 'Quatuor Coronati No. 2076' published annually since 1886, in *Acta Quatuor Coronatorum*, see <quatuorcoronati.com>.

Chris Hodapp, author of *Freemasonry for Dummies* (first published in 2005), runs a blog which provides updated and reliable information about the contemporary world of and debate on freemasonry, see <freemasonryfordummies.com>.

Films

The Scottish Key (2009), a historical documentary by Belgian director Tristan Bourlard investigating the origins of freemasonry. A number of scholars in the field are interviewed.

Terra Masonica (2016), a documentary by Belgian director Tristan Bourlard devoted to mirroring the diversity of contemporary freemasonry across the globe, see <terramasonica.com>.

Museums, archives, and libraries

Most grand lodges host impressive museum, archive, and library collections, and offer visits, arrange special exhibitions, and give guided tours. Their websites facilitate any search for information and display a large number of digitized materials. European institutions are members of the organization AMMLA (<www.ammla.org>); the sister organization in Northern America is called MLMA (<www.masoniclibraries.org>).

The following institutions are particularly recommended for a visit:

Alexandria, VA (USA): George Washington Masonic Memorial, 101 Callahan Drive, Alexandria, Virginia 22301 <https://gwmemorial.org>.

Bayreuth (Germany): Deutsches Freimaurer Museum, Im Hofgarten 1, 95444 Bayreuth, <http://www.freimaurermuseum.de>.

Lexington, MA (USA): Scottish Rite Museum and Library, 33 Marrett Road, Lexington, MA 02421, <http://www.srmml.org>.

London (UK): The Library and Museum of Freemasonry, 60 Great Queen Street, London WC2B 5AZ, <http://freemasonry.london.museum>.

Paris (FR): Musée de la Franc-Maçonnerie, 16 Rue de Cadet, 75009 Paris, <http://www.godf.org/museefm/infos.htm>.

Washington, DC (USA): House of the Temple, 1733 16th St. NW, Washington, DC 20009–3103, <https://scottishrite.org/headquarters/museums/>.

Chapter 1: Two approaches to freemasonry

All references to Tolstoy's *War and Peace* are taken from the searchable open access edition on the website of Project Gutenberg: <http://www.gutenberg.org/files/2600/2600-h/2600-h.htm>.

Stephen Knight, *The Brotherhood: The Secret World of the Freemasons* (Granada, 1983).

Martin Short, *Inside the Brotherhood: Further Secrets of the Freemasons* (Grafton, 1989).

Home Affairs Committee Third Report, 'Freemasonry in the Police and the Judiciary', 19 March 1997, available at: <www.parliament.uk>.

Home Affairs Committee Second Report, 'Freemasonry in Public Life', 19 May 1999, available at: <www.parliament.uk>.

Chapter 2: Three centuries of freemasonry

Andreas Önnerfors and Róbert Péter (eds), *Researching British Freemasonry 1717–2017* (CRFF, 2010).

Andreas Önnerfors and Dorothe Sommer (eds), *Freemasonry and Fraternalism in the Middle East* (CRFF, 2008).

Dorothe Sommer, *Freemasonry in the Ottoman Empire: A History of the Fraternity and Its Influence in Syria and the Levant* (I.B. Tauris, 2015).

Stefan-Ludwig Hoffmann, *The Politics of Sociability: Freemasonry and German Civil Society 1840–1918* (The University of Michigan Press, 2007).

Jessica Harland-Jacobs, *Builders of Empire: Freemasons and British Imperialism, 1717–1927* (The University of North Carolina Press, 2013).

Yves Hivert-Messeca, *L'Europe sous l'acacia. Histoire des franc européennes du XVIIIe siècle à nos jours* (Dervy, 2013–16).
A three-volume history of freemasonry in Europe.

One of the rare sociological and contemporary accounts is J. Scott Kenney, *Brought to Light: Contemporary Freemasonry, Meaning* and *Society* (Wilfried Lauder University Press, 2016) and is also a major reference for the understanding of ritual for contemporary members of freemasonry.

Chapter 3: Historical legacies

John Walker, '"From the Holy Grail and the Ark of the Covenant to Freemasonry and the Priory of Sion": An Introduction to the After-history of the Templars', in P. Edbury (ed.), *The Military Orders*, volume 5 (Farnham, 2012).

Georges Lamoine, 'The Chevalier de Ramsay's Oration 1736–37', *Ars Quatuor Coronatum*, volume 114 (Quatuor Coronati, 2001). This is the first full-text English translation of the influential 'Discours'.

Alain Bernheim, *Ramsay et ses deux discours* (Editions Télètes, 2011) is the most authoritative edition of Ramsay's 'Discours' in French.

Templiers et francs-maçons—de la légende à l'histoire (Musée de la Franc-Maçonnerie, 2016).

'Le surréalisme et le mythe templier', special issue of *La Vertèbre et le Rossignol*, volume 3 (2015).

Chapter 4: Enlightenment foundations

The Constitutions of the Freemasons: Containing the History, Charges, Regulations &c. of that most Ancient and Right Worshipful Fraternity. For the Use of the Lodges (London, 1723).

Georg Simmel (1906), 'The Sociology of Secrecy and of Secret Societies', *American Journal of Sociology* 11(4): 441–98.

Chapter 5: From darkness to light

Henrik Bogdan, *Western Esotericism and Rituals of Initiation* (State University of New York Press, 2007).

Kristiane Hasselmann, 'Die Rituale der Freimaurer. Zur Konstitution eines bürgerlichen Habitus im England des 18. Jahrhunderts' (unpublished manuscript, 2009).

Samuel Prichard, *Masonry Dissected* (London, 1730).

Abbé Perau, *L'Ordre des Franc-Maçons trahi et le secret des Mopses revelée* (Amsterdam, 1745).

Jan Snoek (2003), 'The Evolution of the Hiramic Legend in England and France', *Heredom* 11: 11–53.

Johann Martin Bernigeroth, *Les coutumes des Francs-Macons* (Leipzig, 1745). The first visual exposure of freemasonry in seven engravings.

The Royal Arch degree is referenced from the website of Stichting Argus in the Netherlands, see <stichtingargus.nl>, which has digitized a vast amount of rituals in freemasonry and other fraternal orders and societies.

The Scottish master degree is referenced from the project on the recently decoded 'Copiale'-manuscript, which contains the exposure of masonic degrees, see <http://stp.lingfil.uu.se/~bea/copiale/>.

Charles William Heckethorn, *The Secret Societies of All Ages and Countries* (London, 1875).

Chapter 6: Organizational culture

Margaret C. Jacob, *The Origins of Freemasonry—Facts and Fictions* (University of Pennsylvania Press, 2006).

Lane's masonic records, see <hrionline.ac.uk/lane/> (University of Sheffield).

Chapter 7: Brotherhood challenged

Alexandra Heidle and Jan A.M. Snoek (eds), *Women's Agency and Rituals in Mixed and Female Masonic Orders* (Brill, 2008). Quotes from the female adoption ritual are taken from the English translation of a Swedish manuscript published in full-text in this volume.

Marie-Cécile Révauger and Jaques Lemaire (eds) (2011–12), *Les Femmes et la franc-maçonnerie, des Lumières à nos jours, I. XVIIIe et XIXe siècles, La Pensée et les hommes*, 55(82–3): 191–8.

Máire Fedelma Cross (ed.), *Gender and Fraternal Orders in Europe, 1300–2000* (Palgrave, 2010).

Janet Burke and Margaret C. Jacob, *Les Premières francs-maçonnes au siècle des Lumières* (PUB, 2010).

Chapter 8: Perceptions, prejudices, and persecutions

J.M. Roberts, *The Mythology of the Secret Societies* (Watkins, 2008).

Claus Oberhauser, *Die veschwörungstheoretische Trias: Barruel—Robison—Starck* (StudienVerlag, 2013).

Andreas Önnerfors, 'The Earliest Account of Swedish Freemasonry? *Relation apologique* (1738) revisited', *Ars Quatuor Coronatorum*, volume 124 (Quatuor Coronati, 2014).

Index

Index

SOCIAL MEDIA
Very Short Introduction

Join our community
www.oup.com/vsi

- Join us online at the official Very Short Introductions **Facebook** page.
- Access the thoughts and musings of our authors with our online **blog**.
- Sign up for our monthly **e-newsletter** to receive information on all new titles publishing that month.
- Browse the full range of Very Short Introductions online.
- Read **extracts** from the Introductions for free.
- If you are a teacher or lecturer you can order inspection copies quickly and simply via our website.

ONLINE CATALOGUE
A Very Short Introduction

Our online catalogue is designed to make it easy to find your ideal Very Short Introduction. View the entire collection by subject area, watch author videos, read sample chapters, and download reading guides.

http://global.oup.com/uk/academic/general/vsi_list/

GLOBALIZATION
A Very Short Introduction
Manfred Steger

'Globalization' has become one of the defining buzzwords of our time - a term that describes a variety of accelerating economic, political, cultural, ideological, and environmental processes that are rapidly altering our experience of the world. It is by its nature a dynamic topic - and this *Very Short Introduction* has been fully updated for 2009, to include developments in global politics, the impact of terrorism, and environmental issues. Presenting globalization in accessible language as a multifaceted process encompassing global, regional, and local aspects of social life, Manfred B. Steger looks at its causes and effects, examines whether it is a new phenomenon, and explores the question of whether, ultimately, globalization is a good or a bad thing.

www.oup.com/vsi